I Used to
Know That

Caroline Taggart was born in London of Scottish parents, spent her childhood in New Zealand and went to university in Sheffield. Confused for some time, she has now lived in Pimlico for twenty-five years and thinks of herself as a Londoner, but continues to change allegiance whenever it suits her, particularly during the rugby season.

She has worked in publishing for nearly thirty years, the last eighteen of them as a freelance editor of non-fiction. She has edited innumerable natural history titles, notably Jonathan Scott's *Big Cat Diary* books and the tie-in to the BBC series *Walking with Dinosaurs*, as well as books on gardening, cookery, health, witchcraft, pop music, the Blitz, the D-Day landings, the workings of the House of Commons and the English language. She has also written a handbook for mature students and an encyclopaedia of dogs, and is the editor of *Writer's Market UK 2009*. She has forgotten at least ninety per cent of everything she has ever known about any of these subjects, which makes her an ideal person to write this book.

I Used to Know That

stuff you forgot from school

CAROLINE TAGGART

MICHAEL O'MARA BOOKS LIMITED

First published in Great Britain in 2008 by
Michael O'Mara Books Limited
9 Lion Yard
Tremadoc Road
London SW4 7NQ

A CIP catalogue record for this book is available
from the British Library.

ISBN: 978-1-84317-309-0

3 5 7 9 10 8 6 4

www.mombooks.com

Cover design, text design and typesetting by Ana Bjezancevic

Front-cover lettering by Toby Buchan

Printed and bound in Great Britain by Clays Ltd, St Ives plc

CONTENTS

Introduction   7
Acknowledgements   8

☞ **ENGLISH LANGUAGE**
Parts of speech   9
Synonyms, antonyms and the like   13
Diphthongs   15
Figures of speech (and other devices
    for spicing up your writing)   16
Prosody   19

☞ **ENGLISH LITERATURE**
Shakespeare   21
Charles Dickens   30
Jane Austen   33
The Brontës   37
Poets   38
Foreign authors   46
American classics   51

☞ **MATHS**
Arithmetic   55
Fractions, decimals and percentages   59
Mean, median and mode   63
Measurements   64
Algebra and equations   68
Geometry   75
Trigonometry   80

☞ **SCIENCE**
Biology   82
Chemistry   91
Physics   101

☞ **HISTORY**
Kings and Queens of England/Britain   112
Presidents of the United States   124
British Prime Ministers   129
So what were all those wars about, then?   138
A few more important dates   146
Explorers   148

☞ **GEOGRAPHY**
Continents and countries of the world   152
The United States of America   162
Mountains   166
Oceans   168
Rivers   169
Geological time   170

☞ **GENERAL STUDIES**
World religions   173
Roman numerals   177
The Seven Wonders of the World   178
A bit of classical mythology   179
Some famous artists   180
Some famous composers   185
The planets   190

Bibliography   191

INTRODUCTION

When I started to write this book, I realized that I did in fact remember lots of stuff. But I didn't remember it completely, or necessarily accurately. I knew, for example, that 'The Assyrian came down like a wolf on the fold' was a perfect example of – what? A dactyl or an anapaest? I had to look it up.[1] I remembered a bit about sines and cosines, but had no idea why they were important. I thought I knew what photosynthesis was – until I sat down to explain it.

In the course of talking to other people about what I might include, I discovered two things. One, that everybody I spoke to had been to school. And two, that that was pretty much the only thing they had in common. They had all forgotten completely different things. So, with every conversation, the book seemed to grow longer. One chat with an editor friend sent me rushing to add the active and passive voices to the English Language chapter. Another friend confessed that she had completely forgotten what a square root was (though I have no idea why she suddenly wanted to know). An American I consulted suggested that I include the nicknames of the states of the USA, because this is something that 'every [American] schoolchild knows'. In the end I had to stop discussing it, or this book would just have growed (like Topsy, I s'pect – see p.51).

---

1 Come to think of it, it's a simile, too – see p.18

All of which is a roundabout way of saying that I hope you too will find things here that strike a chord, however faintly.[2] Things that make you say, 'Oh, yes, I used to know that.' Because by the time you read this, I will almost certainly have forgotten most of them again.

Thank you

I'd like to thank Ana, who wanted me to write this book, Silvia, for making it happen and for sharing my loathing of 'Wuthering Heights', and the other Ana, for neck-breaking design. Thanks, also, to everyone who has entered into the spirit of it and made enthusiastic suggestions, even if I haven't had room to include them all. Special thanks to Bob, for vetting the Maths and Science chapters and pointing out that pi wasn't a recurring decimal. I used to know that.

This book is for Jon and Nic, who are old enough to start forgetting this sort of stuff; and for Mishak and Camille, who are just beginning to learn it.

---

2 Or is it a cord?

ENGLISH LANGUAGE

Learning to read and write was just the beginning. After you'd mastered that, you had to find out how the language worked and, when you started to write your own stories, how to use it to better effect. If (perish the thought) you had to write poetry, too, there was a whole new set of conventions…

Parts of speech

This is a way of categorizing words according to the function they perform in a sentence, and there are nine of them.

Noun: a naming word. There are three categories:
- collective nouns, describing a group of things:
  a herd of elephants
- proper nouns, the name of a person, place or whatever that requires a capital letter: *Caroline, Paris, the Smithsonian Institution*
- common nouns, meaning everything else: *street, book, photograph*

Verb: a doing word, or, more accurately, a word that indicates the occurrence or performance of an action, or the existence of a state or condition: *to be, to do, to run, to happen.* This form of a verb (normally containing the word *to*) is called the **infinitive**. Verbs change their form according to tense, person and number: *I am, I was, you were, he is, they are.* Verbs can also be in the **active** or **passive voice** – *I bake the bread* is active, *the bread is baked* is passive. English also has three moods: the **indicative,** making a simple statement (*I bake the bread*); the **subjunctive**, indicating something that is wished or possible (*if I were you, I would bake the bread*); and the **imperative**, used to give a command: *bake that bread!*

Adjective: a describing word: *tall, short, brown, blue.* With rare exceptions such as *blond/blonde*, adjectives in English (unlike most European languages) are invariable; that is, they don't change according to the number and gender of the thing they are describing.

Adverb: where an adjective normally describes a noun, an adverb describes a verb, an adjective or another adverb and answers such questions as how, when or where: *She walked **aimlessly; light** brown hair* (where *light* is an adverb describing the adjective *brown*); *they lived **fairly frugally*** (where *fairly* is an adverb describing the adverb *frugally*). Most but by no means all adverbs in English are formed by adding *-ly* to the adjective.

Pronoun: a word that stands in the place of a noun. Thus: *Caroline has forgotten a lot of stuff. That is why **she** is writing this book* – where the pronoun *she* in the second sentence takes the place of the proper noun *Caroline* in the first.

Conjunction: a joining word: *and, but, though* and so on, linking two words, phrases or clauses together: Pride **and** Prejudice *is Jane Austen's most popular book,* **but** *I also love* Sense **and** Sensibility, ***though*** *Marianne can be really annoying.*

Preposition: a word placed in front of a noun or pronoun to shows its relationship to another part of the sentence. Preposi-tions are normally little words such as *at, in* or *on: The boy stood* **on** *the burning deck; it was Greek* **to** *me.*

Interjection: a word thrown in to express emotion, such as *aha!* or *alas!*

Article: *Collins English Dictionary* defines an article as 'a kind of determiner... that lacks independent meaning but may serve to indicate the specificity of the noun phrase with which it occurs'. That's not very helpful, is it? It may be easier just to remember that the definite article is *the* and the indefinite articles are *a* and *an.*

Mentioning clauses and phrases suggests that it may be time for a few more definitions:
- A **phrase** is a group of words (in a sentence) that does not contain a verb.
- A **clause** does contain a verb and may be a whole sentence or part of a sentence (when it is often called a **subordinate clause**).
- Sentences – and each clause of a sentence – can be divided into **subject** and **predicate**.

* The **subject** is the noun or noun phrase that the sentence is about, the thing that does the action expressed in the verb.
* The **predicate** is everything else. In sentences involving the verb *to be*, what follows the verb is known as the **complement**, as in *Silence is golden*, where *golden* is the complement of the verb.
* A verb may be **transitive** or **intransitive**, which means it may or may not need a direct object in order to make sense. The object is the thing on which the subject performs the action of the verb: *he hit **the ball**.*

To see some examples of all this, let's look at a line from *A Midsummer Night's Dream:*

> *I know a bank whereon the wild thyme blows*

The main statement or principal clause is *I know a bank*. Not very interesting, but it stands alone as a sentence. *I* is the subject, *know a bank* is the predicate and can be subdivided into the verb *know* and the object (answering the question 'What do I know?'), *a bank*. *Know* in this sentence is a transitive verb – it doesn't make much sense without the object.

The subordinate clause is *whereon the wild thyme blows*. It's got a verb (*blows*), with a subject (*the wild thyme,* which is a noun phrase), but isn't a sentence. Note, however, that *blows* makes sense on its own – it doesn't need an object, so it is intransitive.

Blow is one of many verbs that can be either transitive or intransitive, depending on context: the wind blows intransitively, but you can blow a horn or blow glass in a transitive way.

And what we have just done to that sentence is called **parsing** – taking it apart to analyse its components.

☞ **A BIT MORE ON COLLECTIVE NOUNS**

Collective nouns are funny things. There are some genuinely useful ones to describe animals that live in groups – you wouldn't talk about a gaggle of elephants, for example, or a flock of lions. But at some stage in our history, someone has thought fit to give collective names to almost a hundred birds where you might have thought that *group*, *colony* or *a whole bunch* would serve the purpose. And there are many variations – if you are talking about a group of ducks, for example, you could say an *adelynge, brace, bunch, dopping, flock, paddling, plump, raft, safe, skein, sord, string* or *team*. *A charm of goldfinches, an exaltation of larks* and *a parliament of owls* or *of rooks* are often quoted but rarely used in real life – but once you start googling for this sort of thing you also come across *a dopping of goosanders*. (Goosanders? Who decided we need a collective noun for goosanders?)

Synonyms, antonyms and the like

The suffix *-nym* derives from the Greek for *name*, but in fact we use these words to refer to meaning. So a **synonym** is a word that has the same or similar meaning as another, while an **antonym** has the opposite meaning.

Illogically, a **homonym** is a word that has the same spelling as another, but a different meaning. A **homophone** sounds like another word, but doesn't have the same spelling. Confused? Here are some examples:

> *Spooky, scary, frightening, eerie* are synonyms, as are *pale, wan, ashen*
>
> *Mean* is an antonym of *generous*
>
> *Fair* is an antonym of *dark*
>
> *Fast* is an antonym of *slow* (or *slowly*)

English abounds in homonyms and homophones, which are often completely unrelated in the etymological sense. There are quite a few in the above examples.

> *Eerie* (spooky) is a homophone of *eyrie* (an eagle's nest)
>
> *Pale* (light in colour) is a homonym of *pale* (a fence, as in *beyond the pale*) and a homophone of *pail* (a bucket)
>
> *Mean* (miserly) is a homonym of *mean* (intend) and a homophone of *mien* (appearance)
>
> *Fair* (light in colour) is a homonym of *fair* (a place that has dodgem cars) and a homophone of *fare* (what you pay on the bus)
>
> *Fast* (quickly) is a homonym of *fast* (giving up eating)

All those silly mistakes that spellcheckers fail to pick up, such as *there/their*, are homophones.

Diphthongs

Diphthongs are complicated things because what most of us think of as a diphthong is actually a digraph or ligature, and true diphthongs are often written as a single letter, so we don't recognize them as such.

Huh?

OK. *Collins English Dictionary* defines a diphthong as 'a vowel sound occupying a single syllable, during the articulation of which the tongue moves from one position to another, causing a continual change in vowel quality, as in the pronunciation of *a* in English *late*, during which the tongue moves from the position of (e) towards (i)'.

Honestly, that's what it says. Try it for yourself and feel the difference when you say *late* and *bat*.

Diphthongs may be written as a single letter (the *i* in *white* and the *o* in *no*, for example) or as two (*ui* in *fruit*, *ea* in *heat*). Any combination of two letters, whether vowels or consonants, which produces a single sound is known as a *digraph*, so that includes not only the *ui* in *fruit* and the *ea* in *heat* but also the *ph* in *photograph* and the *dg* in bridge.

The *ae* written together in *encyclopaedia* or the *oe* in *amoeba* is, strictly speaking, a ligature, which means that the two letters are joined together as one. This has its origins with medieval scribes who were simply trying to save time and space, and was later transferred to hot metal type, where the two letters would appear on the same 'sort' or block. Modern typesetting doesn't really do ligatures, so the tendency since the 1950s has been to write the two letters separately, or increasingly to drop one of them altogether – with the result that, in British English, *encyclopaedia* and *mediaeval* look rather old-fashioned while, in American English, *ameba* and *estrogen* have become standard spellings.

Figures of speech (and other devices for spicing up your writing)

A figure of speech is technically an expression such as a **metaphor**, in which a word is used in a non-literal (that is, a figurative) way, as when you say *My lips are sealed* – because, unless you have put glue over them, they are nothing of the sort. But when we were studying these things they were always expanded to include such devices as **alliteration** and **onomatopoeia**, which poets also used for effect. Here are some of the ones I remember:

alliteration: when a number of words in quick succession begin with the same letter, or the same letter is repeated: *Full fathom five thy father lies*, as Ariel sings in *The Tempest*.

assonance: similar to alliteration, but this time repeating vowel sounds:

> *That solitude which suits*
> *Abstruser musings*
> (Coleridge, *Frost at Midnight*)

euphemism: replacing an unpleasant word or concept with something less offensive, as in *the Grim Reaper* for *death*, and various alternatives to swear words and matters sexual.

hyperbole: Pronounced hy-PER-bo-lee. Not hyper-bowl. Exaggeration for effect, as in *I've told you a hundred times*. The opposite of…

litotes: understatement for effect, as when *not bad* means *completely wonderful*.

metaphor: an expression in which a word is used in a non-literal sense, saying that *x is y*, rather than *x is like y*, which would be a simile (see below). So, for example, Macbeth's

Life's but a walking shadow, a poor player,
That struts and frets his hour upon the stage

metonymy: Fowler's *Modern English Usage* (a book no self-respecting pedant should be without) defines this as 'substitution of an attributive or other suggestive word for the name of the thing meant', as *Downing Street* or *Washington* are used to mean *the British Prime Minister* or *the US government*. Easily confused with synecdoche (see below).

onomatopoeia: a word or phrase that sounds (a bit) like the sound it is meant to convey: *buzz, purr,* or Tennyson's *the murmuring of innumerable bees.*

oxymoron: an apparent contradiction for effect, the classic example being *bitter sweet.*

personification: giving human qualities to an inanimate object or an abstract idea: Keats's *To Autumn* is personification from start to finish, as he is addressing the season as if it were a person:

> *Close bosom-friend of the maturing sun;*
> *Conspiring with him how to load and bless*
> *With fruit the vines that round the thatch-eaves run*

If I had written, 'addressing the season as if *she* were a person', that would have been personification, too.[3]

simile: a comparison that – unlike a metaphor – expresses itself as a comparison, usually with the words *as* or *like*: *as dead as a dodo, like a bat out of hell.*

synecdoche: a form of metonymy, but in this instance specifically 'a whole for the part or a part for the whole': as with *England* meaning *the English football team*, or the television programme *New Faces*, which isn't intended to imply that the contestants have left their bodies at home.

---

3 Never personify inanimate objects – they don't like it.

Prosody

Confusingly, prosody has nothing to do with prose – it is defined by *Collins* as 'the study of poetic metre and of the art of versification, including rhyme, stanzaic forms, and the quantity and stress of syllables'.

The basic unit of a line of poetry – normally comprising two or three syllables – is called a **foot**, and the most common feet are:

iamb (adj. **iambic**): a short syllable followed by a long one. The most widely used foot in English poetry. Much of Shakespeare's verse is written in *iambic pentameters*, which means that a line consists of five iambic feet, or ten syllables in all:

Shall I /compare/ thee to/ a sum/mer's day?
(*Sonnet 43*)

If mu/sic be/ the food/ of love,/ play on
(*Twelfth Night*)

trochee: a long syllable followed by a short one, although the final syllable is often missing:

Tyger!/ Tyger!/ burning/ bright
In the/ forest /of the/ night
(Blake, *The Tyger*)

dactyl: a long syllable followed by two short ones (again, the final syllable is often dropped): it produces a gentle, flowing rhythm:

> This is the/ forest prim/eval. The/ murmuring/
> pines and the/ hemlocks
> (Longfellow, *Evangeline*)

anapaest: two short syllables followed by a long one. In contrast to a dactyl, this conveys pace and action:

> The Assyr/ian came down/ like a wolf/ on the fold
> (Byron, *The Destruction of Sennacherib*)

> I sprang/ to the stir/rup and Jo/ris and he,
> I gal/loped, Dirk gal/loped, we gal/loped all three
> (Browning, *How They Brought the Good News from Ghent to Aix*)

spondee: two long syllables, giving a heavy, rhythmical effect: this example combines spondee and trochee so that you can almost hear the soldiers plodding along:

> We're /foot—slog/—slog—slog/
> —sloggin'/ over/ Africa—
> Foot—foot/—foot—foot/—sloggin'/ over/ Africa—
> (Boots—boots/—boots—boots/—movin'/ up and/
> down a/gain!)
> (Kipling, *Boots*)

ENGLISH LITERATURE

Oh, those dreadful set texts. The fact that I had to study *Sons and Lovers* for O Level is the reason that D. H. Lawrence doesn't get a mention in this book (other than that one, of course) – I've never recovered. On the other hand, I did *Macbeth* twice and loved every minute of it, and I still happily re-read *Great Expectations*, so maybe even at fifteen I was just too cynical for Lawrence. Anyway, here are some of the texts that may or may not have made your life a misery all those years ago.

Shakespeare

William Shakespeare (1564–1616) wrote thirty-seven plays, 154 sonnets and a number of much longer poems, of which the best known is *Venus and Adonis*. There isn't room in this book to summarize all the plays, so here are – arguably – the twelve best known.

☞ TWELFTH NIGHT
Subtitled *What You Will*. Twins Viola and Sebastian are separated in a storm and each believes the other dead. Viola disguises herself as a boy, Cesario, and enters the service of Duke Orsino, with whom she falls in love. Orsino, however, is

in love with Olivia and uses Cesario as a messenger to woo her. Olivia – you guessed it – falls in love with Cesario, and it takes the reappearance of Sebastian to make everyone live happily ever after. The subplot concerns Olivia's pompous steward, Malvolio, who is conned by Olivia's uncle and his friends into believing that Olivia is in love with him and wishes to see him wearing yellow stockings and cross garters. The bit about 'some are born great, some achieve greatness and some have greatness thrust upon them' appears in the letter that Malvolio believes Olivia has written to him.

☞ THE TAMING OF THE SHREW

Katharina is too bad-tempered to get a husband, but her father will not allow her younger (and better behaved) sister, Bianca, to accept any of her many suitors until Katharina is married. Petruchio comes along and accepts the challenge, more or less literally beating Kate into submission. Twenty-first century feminists do not care for this play, although Cole Porter's musical version, *Kiss Me Kate*, is wonderful.

☞ A MIDSUMMER NIGHT'S DREAM

The one about the fairies. Three plots interwoven: in a wood outside Athens, two pairs of young lovers brush up against the squabbling king and queen of the fairies, Oberon and Titania, and Oberon's servant Puck. In the same wood, a group of workmen, including Bottom the Weaver, are rehearsing the play *Pyramus and Thisbe* to perform at the forthcoming wedding of the Duke of Athens. Oberon has a magic potion which, when squeezed on the eyelids of someone who is asleep, makes them fall in love with the first object they see when they wake up. As a result, Titania falls in love with Bottom, whom Puck has given an ass's head, and Puck confuses the young lovers so that they keep falling in and out of love with the wrong partners. But it all comes right in the end.

☞ THE MERCHANT OF VENICE

Shylock the Jewish moneylender hates Antonio the Christian merchant; when Antonio needs to borrow money from him to help out his friend Bassanio, Shylock makes him sign a bond promising that he will pay Shylock one pound of his own flesh should he fail to repay the loan. Bassanio takes the money and successfully courts the wealthy Portia. Antonio's ships are lost at sea and he is unable to pay Shylock, who claims his pound of flesh. Portia disguises herself as a lawyer and rescues Antonio by pointing out that, contractually, Shylock is entitled to take a pound of flesh but no blood – a logistical impossibility. Her speech beginning 'The quality of mercy is not strained' comes from this scene. A happy ending – unless you are Shylock.

☞ ROMEO AND JULIET

The original star-crossed lovers. Romeo is a Montague, Juliet a Capulet and the two families hate each other. Romeo and Juliet secretly marry. Then, in one of those clever schemes that you just know are going to go wrong, Juliet takes a potion that will put her into a coma for a couple of days, so that everyone thinks she is dead and she won't have to marry her cousin, Paris. The message telling Romeo about this goes astray (of course) and he arrives at her tomb, believing that she is dead. He poisons himself just before she wakes up, discovers him dead and stabs herself with his dagger.

The balcony scene is full of famous lines: Romeo is lurking in the garden when Juliet appears on the balcony above and, talking to herself, says:

> O Romeo, Romeo! wherefore art thou Romeo?...
> What's in a name? That which we call a rose,
> By any other word would smell as sweet.

And at the end of the scene, she says:

> Good-night, good-night! parting is such sweet sorrow
> That I shall say good-night till it be morrow.

~~~~~~

☞ **KING HENRY V**

Shakespeare's greatest rabble-rousing work, full of stuff like 'God for Harry, England and Saint George!' and the fabulous speech about tomorrow being St Crispian's Day. The battle of Agincourt (see p.139) is the centrepiece of the play, which ends with Henry marrying the French king's daughter in order to bring peace between England and France.

☞ THE LIFE AND DEATH OF KING RICHARD III

Don't get me started. A noxious piece of Tudor propaganda, which turned Richard into the murderous hunchback of popular myth. Good quotes, though – it starts with:

> *Now is the winter of our discontent*
> *Made glorious summer by this sun of York.*[4]

and ends (more or less) with:

> *A horse! a horse! My kingdom for a horse!*

☞ KING LEAR

Lear is 'the foolish, fond old man' who decides to retire and divide his kingdom between his three daughters, Goneril, Regan and Cordelia. The two eldest make fancy speeches about loving their father above all else; Cordelia refuses to play this game and is promptly exiled (did I mention Lear was foolish?). Lear plans to spend half his time with Goneril and half with Regan, but these two wicked sisters have other ideas and soon turf him out of doors. He wanders around in the rain, goes mad, meets up with Cordelia again and then everyone dies. There is a subplot concerning the Duke of Gloster's bastard son Edmund, who plots against everyone and becomes betrothed to both Goneril and Regan (despite the fact that they are both married). They all die, too.

---

4 Meaning his brother, who has just become King Edward IV. It's a pun, because Edward is also a son of the House of York.

☞ JULIUS CAESAR

A number of Roman citizens, notably Caesar's close friend Marcus Brutus and his brother-in-law, Cassius, are worried that Caesar is becoming too powerful, so they kill him ('Et tu, Brute? Then fall Caesar'). But that happens in Act III scene I, only halfway through the play. The rest is about the fall-out from the assassination: the vengeance wrought on the conspirators by Caesar's supporters, led by Mark Antony; the conflict between Brutus and Cassius (the one who has 'a lean and hungry look – he thinks too much, such men are dangerous'); the effect on them of their feelings of guilt; and their eventual defeat and suicide. And speaking of rabble-rousing, Antony's funeral oration, working the crowd up into a frenzy so that they will avenge the murder, runs anything in *Henry V* pretty close:

> Friends, Romans, countrymen; lend me your ears;
> I come to bury Caesar, not to praise him...
> He was my friend, faithful and just to me:
> But Brutus says he was ambitious;
> And Brutus is an honourable man...

and so on and so forth, until the mob is fairly baying for Brutus's blood.

☞ MACBETH

The Scottish play. Three witches prophesy that Macbeth will become Thane of Cawdor and subsequently king. When he is proclaimed Thane of Cawdor, he starts wondering about hurrying the second prophecy along. Egged on by his wife, he murders King Duncan and is proclaimed king in his place. And it's all downhill from there. One murder leads to another, he is haunted by guilt (personified by the ghost of his friend Banquo, who appears at a banquet), Lady Macbeth goes mad and dies (after the famous 'Out damned spot' hand-washing/sleepwalking scene), Macbeth is finally killed in battle and Duncan's son Malcolm is restored to the throne.

☞ HAMLET, PRINCE OF DENMARK

Another one where everyone dies. Hamlet's father, also Hamlet, has died in suspicious circumstances and his widow, Gertrude, has married – with indecent haste – Hamlet Senior's brother, Claudius. The ghost of King Hamlet tells his son that he has been murdered by Claudius. Prince Hamlet then spends much of the play worrying about what to do and talking to himself – hence all the famous soliloquies. He has previously been attached to Ophelia, daughter of Polonius, the lord chamberlain, but he now rejects her ('Get thee to a nunnery'). Talking to his mother in her room, Hamlet realizes that someone is eavesdropping behind an arras and stabs him, believing it to be Claudius. It is in fact Polonius. Ophelia goes mad and drowns herself. Her brother, Laertes, is determined to avenge his family, so Claudius arranges a fencing match in which Laertes will have a poisoned sword. Laertes wounds Hamlet, then there is a scuffle in which the two exchange swords and Hamlet wounds Laertes. Knowing that he is dying, Laertes confesses, Hamlet stabs Claudius and Gertrude drinks poisoned wine that Claudius had prepared as a fallback position for getting rid of Hamlet. 'Good night, sweet prince,' says his friend Horatio as he prepares to clear up the mess.

Hamlet is fuller of quotations than the other plays, so here are just a couple: Polonius's paternal advice to his son Laertes:

> Neither a borrower nor a lender be:
> For loan oft loses both itself and friend;
> And borrowing dulls the edge of husbandry.
> This above all – to thine own self be true;
> And it must follow, as the night the day,
> Thou canst not then be false to any man.

And a bit of Hamlet's most famous soliloquy:

> To be, or not to be; that is the question:
> Whether 'tis nobler in the mind to suffer
> The slings and arrows of outrageous fortune,
> Or to take arms against a sea of troubles,
> And by opposing end them? To die, to sleep;
> No more; and by a sleep to say we end
> The heart-ache and the thousand natural shocks
> That flesh is heir to, — 'tis a consummation
> Devoutly to be wish'd. To die, to sleep;
> To sleep! perchance to dream: ay, there's the rub;
> For in that sleep of death what dreams may come,
> When we have shuffled off this mortal coil,
> Must give us pause.

At a rough count, six quotations in thirteen lines. Not bad.

☞ **OTHELLO, THE MOOR OF VENICE**

Othello is a successful general, but the problem is that he is black and has secretly married a white girl, Desdemona. The other problem is that Iago hates him, partly because Othello has promoted a young lieutenant, Cassio, over Iago's head. Iago persuades Othello that Cassio is having an affair with Desdemona. Mad with jealousy ('the green-eyed monster'), Othello smothers Desdemona in her bed. Iago also tries to have Cassio murdered, but the plot goes wrong and letters proving Iago's guilt and Cassio's innocence are discovered. Othello realises that he has murdered Desdemona for no reason, and kills himself. Othello was the man who loved 'not wisely but too well', and it was Iago who said, 'Who steals my purse steals trash.' (But he was lying, of course.)

Oh, and here's a smattering of one famous sonnet – number 43 – whose first four lines have provided titles for at least two novels:

> *Shall I compare thee to a summer's day?*
> *Thou are more lovely and more temperate;*
> *Rough winds do shake the darling buds of May,*
> *And summer's lease hath all too short a date.*

Charles Dickens

Love him or hate him (and most people do one or the other), he's inspired a lot of great films and everyone knows what *Dickensian* means. Three of his most enduring novels are:

☞ DAVID COPPERFIELD

Dickens's favourite (and mine too, although *Our Mutual Friend* is a close second) – the life story of a boy who is sent to boarding school by his evil stepfather, runs away to his eccentric aunt, becomes a lawyer and then a writer. Sounds pretty dull, but really it is about growing up, learning from experience and coming to terms with life – which makes it sound pompous, but it isn't a bit. It's full of characters we all remember – Mr Micawber, always hoping that something will turn up; the ever so 'umble Uriah Heep; Aunt Betsy Trotwood and her mad companion Mr Dick, who is obsessed with the execution of Charles I; the Peggotty family, the deeply drippy Dora and the saintly Agnes.

☞ OLIVER TWIST

About the boy from the workhouse who is kicked out after he 'wants some more' food and finds his way into a gang of pickpockets led by Fagin. The novel contains considerably more misery and rather less singing and dancing than the musical version.

☞ A CHRISTMAS CAROL

The miserly Ebenezer Scrooge tries to ignore Christmas and is haunted by the ghost of his former partner, Marley, and by the ghosts of Christmases Past, Present and Yet to Come, who show him the error of his ways.

If you don't remember much about Dickens, chances are most of the characters you do recall are from those three – the ones mentioned above from *David Copperfield*; the Artful Dodger, Nancy, the evil Bill Sikes and Mr Bumble the beadle from *Oliver Twist*; Bob Cratchit and Tiny Tim from *A Christmas Carol*. But here are a few more that may ring bells:

📖

The arch-hypocrite Mr Pecksniff and his daughters, Charity and Mercy, from *Martin Chuzzlewit*, which also has the drunken nurse Sarah Gamp (possibly the only character in literature to have an umbrella named after her).

📖

Sydney Carton, who dies by the guillotine in *A Tale of Two Cities*, saying, 'It is a far, far better thing that I do, than I have ever done…' *A Tale of Two Cities* also features Madame Defarge and her wonderfully named friend The Vengeance, clicking their knitting needles to count the heads as they roll.

📖

Little Nell in *The Old Curiosity Shop* – best known because Oscar Wilde said that you would have to have a heart of stone to read about her death without laughing. She certainly spends most of the novel sobbing and you are glad to see the back of her, frankly.

Pip (Philip Pirrip), the central character in *Great Expectations*, which also contains mad Miss Havisham, still wearing the wedding dress from the day she was jilted many years ago; the beautiful Estella, brought up by Miss Havisham to wreak her revenge on the male sex; the convict Abel Magwitch; Pip's friend Herbert Pocket and the lawyer's clerk Mr Wemmick with his eccentric Aged Parent.

📖

Mr Squeers, the headmaster of the infamous Dotheboys Hall in *Nicholas Nickleby*, and Smike, his doomed pupil.

📖

Mr Pickwick, of course, from *The Pickwick Papers*. His fellow members of the Pickwick Club are Messrs Tracy Tupman, Augustus Snodgrass and Nathaniel Winkle, and his faithful servant is Sam Weller, who contributed to the English language the concept of the Wellerism – a statement along the lines of 'It's over, and can't be helped, and that's one consolation, as they always say in Turkey, ven they cut the wrong man's head off'.

📖

The plot of *Bleak House* centres round the ongoing case of Jarndyce vs. Jarndyce, which eventually eats up all the money that is being disputed; the Circumlocution Office, Dickens' savage attack on civil service bureaucracy, appears in *Little Dorrit*; and *Barnaby Rudge* is set against the background of the Gordon Riots (although I don't think I ever knew what *they* were)[5].

---

5 Just looked them up. They were anti-Catholic riots in London in 1780, stirred up by Lord George Gordon. So now we know.

Jane Austen

Jane Austen completed only six novels, which makes it easy to do a run-down of her entire oeuvre. In no particular order:

☞ PRIDE AND PREJUDICE

Spirited but poor Elizabeth Bennet takes against the proud but very rich Mr Darcy, particularly when he destroys the chances of her sister Jane marrying his friend Mr Bingley. Darcy falls in love with Lizzy much against his better judgement and is tactless enough to tell her so. Scandal hits the Bennet family when youngest daughter Lydia elopes with the charming but feckless Wickham, but Darcy saves the day. An unlikely scenario for bringing lovers together, but it does and the two 'deserving' daughters make the happy marriages we have predicted all along.

Other characters include two more Bennet sisters, plain and studious Mary and silly Kitty, and their parents, the empty-headed Mrs Bennet and reclusive, sarcastic Mr Bennet; Mr Bennet's cousin and heir, the obsequious clergyman Mr Collins, and his haughty patroness Lady Catherine de Bourgh, who also happens to be Darcy's aunt.

☞ EMMA

Emma Woodhouse is the most important young lady in her village, living alone with her valetudinarian father (the one who thinks that the sooner any party breaks up the better). Clever and pleased with herself, she amuses herself with matchmaking; to the disapproval of her friend and neighbour, Mr Knightley, she persuades her protégée, Harriet Smith, not to marry a respectable farmer, Robert Martin, thinking that Harriet (despite being poor, ignorant and illegitimate) should set her sights on the new vicar, Mr Elton. Mr Elton, however, has set his sights on Emma, and is deeply offended when she rejects him. He promptly marries someone else entirely, and Harriet, recovering from her disappointment, falls in love with Mr Knightley instead. Emma's eyes are suddenly opened to the fact that no one should marry Mr Knightley but herself. Fortunately, this turns out to be what he has always wanted.

☞ SENSE AND SENSIBILITY

The Dashwood sisters, Elinor and Marianne, are completely different in temperament, and, when Marianne falls in love with the dashing Willoughby, the whole world knows it. Elinor, on the other hand, suffers her disappointment over Edward Ferrars in silence. Willoughby is called up to London just as he appears to be on the brink of proposing to Marianne and becomes engaged to a wealthy woman. Marianne's heartbreak is eventually healed by the less dashing Colonel Brandon and Elinor gets Edward in the end.

☞ NORTHANGER ABBEY

Catherine Morland's head is full of ghoulish Gothic novels, so when she is invited to Northanger Abbey by her friend Elinor Tilney (with whose brother Henry she is already in love), she thinks she has discovered a horrific mystery: Elinor's father, the general, has murdered his wife. It turns out to be nonsense, of course, and she is deeply embarrassed that Henry should know of her silly suspicions. General Tilney now discovers that Catherine is not, as he has been led to believe, an heiress, and turns her out of the house. She is back at home thinking gloomy thoughts about her future when Henry appears and…

☞ MANSFIELD PARK

Jane Austen's least appealing heroine is the virtuous but dull dull dull Fanny Price, who is sent to live at Mansfield Park with her aunt, Lady Bertram, and promptly falls in love with her cousin Edmund, another deeply virtuous person. The arrival of the worldly Crawfords, brother and sister Henry and Mary, upsets the calm of the neighbourhood, with Edmund becoming smitten with Mary, despite his disapproval of her character, and Henry attracting the attention of both Bertram sisters, despite the fact that both have admirers of their own. Henry, however, falls in love with Fanny, who is almost persuaded that her good influence can redeem his character, but then he elopes with Maria Bertram, now Mrs Rushworth. Amid all the scandal and disappointment, Edmund finally recognizes Fanny's worth.

☞ PERSUASION

Eight years before the novel starts, Anne Elliot was persuaded by her proud father, Sir Walter, and her well-meaning friend Lady Russell to break off her engagement to Captain Frederick Wentworth. Now twenty-six, she has never met anyone else she can care for (and indeed has turned down a proposal from a neighbour, Charles Musgrove, who has subsequently married her sister, Mary). Chance brings Captain Wentworth, now wealthy, back into the neighbourhood, but throws him together with Charles Musgrove's sisters, Henrietta and Louisa. Anne is forced to watch in silence as he apparently becomes involved with Louisa, whose steadfastness of character seems to appeal to him more than the weakness he has not forgiven in Anne. An outing to Lyme Regis ends with Louisa insisting on jumping off the Cobb, falling and causing herself serious injury. Just as Captain Wentworth's feelings towards Anne are reawakening, he finds that all his friends believe he is committed to Louisa, and he cannot honourably renege on this perceived promise. But Louisa, in the course of her convalescence, conveniently falls in love with Captain Wentworth's friend Captain Benwick, and Wentworth is free again.

Jane Austen also wrote fragments of two other novels, *The Watsons* and *Sanditon*, which have been published in their incomplete forms and variously completed by other authors.

The Brontës

There were three sisters who wrote novels – Charlotte, Emily and Anne. All, especially Emily, were also poets of some distinction. Charlotte wrote *Shirley*, *Villette* and *The Professor*, but her most famous novel is:

☞ **JANE EYRE**

Poor orphan gets a job as governess to the ward of Mr Rochester at Thornfield Hall, a place where strange noises tend to emanate from the attic. Jane and Rochester fall in love but their wedding is stopped by the intervention of Mr Mason, who announces that Rochester is in fact married to his sister, Bertha. And indeed he is: but she is mad and confined to the attic, watched over by fearsome Grace Poole. Jane runs away and seeks refuge with her cousins, the Rivers; on the point of accepting a proposal of marriage from St John Rivers, she thinks she hears Rochester calling her and insists on returning to Thornfield. There she finds that Bertha has broken out of her attic, set fire to the house, perished in the flames and left Rochester blind, disfigured and dependent. 'Reader,' as she famously says, 'I married him.'

Emily wrote only one novel:

☞ **WUTHERING HEIGHTS**

Heathcliff and Cathy, you've heard the song. I'm going to stick my neck out here and say that this has got to be the most overrated novel of all time. Heathcliff is a wild orphan brought home to Wuthering Heights by kindly Mr Earnshaw, Cathy's father. The two fall passionately in love, but Cathy refuses to marry a nobody and instead marries their drippy neighbour, Edgar Linton. Heathcliff, in revenge, marries Edgar's sister, Isabella, and cruelly mistreats her. Cathy dies in childbirth... Do I need to go on? Oh OK, Heathcliff goes a bit bonkers and ends up pretty much killing himself so as to be reunited with Cathy in death.

Anne's only two novels are *Agnes Gray* (substantially auto-biographical, about the horrors of being a governess in Victorian England) and *The Tenant of Wildfell Hall*, about a woman, Helen Graham, with a murky past.

Poets

I always found that there was nothing like studying a poem to kill it stone dead, so I avoided poetry as much as possible for many years. Even if you did the same, you were probably force fed some of the following (many of whom I belatedly realize are well worth reading):

☞ **GEOFFREY CHAUCER** (*c*.1345–1400, English)
The first great poet in English, although his language is pretty unfamiliar to the uninitiated. Best known for *The Canterbury Tales*, in which a party of outrageous pilgrims travel from the

Tabard Inn in Southwark, London, to Canterbury Cathedral and tell stories to pass the time. The prologue presents a vivid portrait of fourteenth-century life; among the best known tellers of tales are the Knight, the Miller, the Man of Law and the Wife of Bath.

☞ **EDMUND SPENSER** (*c*.1552–99, English)

Author of *The Faerie Queene* and the single most important reason that Doctor Johnson decided to invent spelling.

☞ **JOHN DONNE** (1572–1631, English)

The greatest of the metaphysical poets (a loose term for a group of seventeenth-century poets whose work investigated the world using intellect rather than intuition, apparently). His most famous line, 'No man is an Island, entire of itself', oft misquoted, is from a book of devotions rather than a poem.

☞ **JOHN MILTON** (1608–74, English)

Puritan, went blind, wrote a sonnet about it. Also the author of *Paradise Lost* and *Paradise Regained*. *Paradise Lost* contains a reference to 'His dark materials', and was the inspiration for Philip Pullman's trilogy of the same name.

☞ **THOMAS GRAY** (1717–71, English)

Gets a mention here because we all read his *Elegy Written in a*

Country Churchyard:

> The curfew tolls the knell of parting day,
> The lowing herd wind slowly o'er the lea,
> The plowman homeward plods his weary way,
> And leaves the world to darkness and to me.

If you only wrote one poem in your life, you'd be quite happy with that one, I'd say.[6]

☞ **ROBERT BURNS** (1759–96, determinedly Scottish)
His birthday was 25 January and for some reason we celebrate it by eating haggis and reciting his poetry. In addition to the wonderfully bloodthirsty *Address to the Haggis*, he also wrote *To a Mouse* ('Wee sleekit, cow'rin' tim'rous beastie' and 'The best laid schemes o' mice an' men/ Gang aft a-gley') and the words of *Auld Lang Syne*.

☞ **WILLIAM WORDSWORTH** (1770–1850, English)
The most important of the Lake Poets (the others were Coleridge and Robert Southey). I have to say I think 'prolix' rather than 'prolific' is the *mot juste* for Wordsworth. He churned it out and goodness he was dull. The far-too-

---

6 To be fair, there are four poems by Gray in the *Oxford Book of English Verse*, one of them the endearingly named *On a Favourite Cat, Drowned in a Tub of Gold Fishes*.

often-quoted *Daffodils* ('I wander'd lonely as a cloud')is one of his, as is the *Sonnet Written on Westminster Bridge* ('Earth hath not anything to show more fair').

☞ **SAMUEL TAYLOR COLERIDGE** (1772–1834, English)
Only two famous poems and one of them unfinished, but what crackers they were: *The Rime of the Ancient Mariner* (that's the one about the wedding guest and the albatross) and *Kubla Khan* ('In Xanadu did Kubla Khan/ A stately pleasure-dome decree'). His friend Wordsworth could have learned a useful lesson about quality versus quantity.

☞ **GEORGE GORDON BYRON, LORD BYRON**
   (1788–1824, English/Scottish)
The one who 'awoke one morning and found myself famous' after the publication of *Childe Harold's Pilgrimage*. He led a wild life, left England after one scandal too many, lived in Italy where he was friendly with Shelley, then fought for Greek insurgents against the Turks. He died at Missolonghi, in Greece, of rheumatic fever contracted after he was soaked in an open boat.

☞ **PERCY BYSSHE SHELLEY** (1792–1822, English)
One of the great Romantic poets, married to Mary, the author of *Frankenstein*. Lived mostly in Europe, latterly Italy, where he was drowned in a boating accident. Author of *Ode to a*

Skylark ('Hail to thee, blithe Spirit!'), *Ozymandias* ('Look on my works, ye Mighty, and despair!') and *Adonais*, an elegy on the death of Keats.

☞ **JOHN KEATS** (1795–1821, English)
Another great Romantic, he's the one who died at the intimidatingly young age of twenty-six of consumption in Rome – you can visit his house, by the Spanish Steps. *La Belle Dame Sans Merci* ('O what can ail thee, knight-at-arms/ Alone and palely loitering?'), *Ode to a Nightingale* ('My heart aches, and a drowsy numbness pains/ My sense, as though of hemlock I had drunk'), *On First Looking into Chapman's Homer* ('Much have I travelled in the realms of gold') and *To Autumn* ('Season of mists and mellow fruitfulness').

☞ **ALFRED LORD TENNYSON** (1809–92, English)
Another prolific one. His great work is *In Memoriam*, written on the early death of his friend Arthur Hallam; but most people are probably more familiar with *Come into the garden, Maud* and *The Lady of Shalott*:

> *Out flew the web and floated wide;*
> *The mirror crack'd from side to side;*
> *'The curse is come upon me!' cried*
> *The Lady of Shalott*

which has caused adolescent schoolgirls to giggle ever since.

☞ **WALT WHITMAN** (1819–92, American)

The great American poet of the nineteenth century; his masterwork is *Leaves of Grass*, a massive collection of short poems, including *O Captain! My Captain!* and *When Lilacs Last in the Dooryard Bloom'd*, both from the section *Memories of President Lincoln*, inspired by the president's assassination.

☞ **RUDYARD KIPLING** (1865–1936, English)

Prolific chronicler of the soldier's lot in South Africa and India, but best known for *If*:

> If you can keep your head while all about you
>   Are losing theirs and blaming it on you...
> If you can meet with Triumph and Disaster
> And treat those two impostors just the same...
> Yours is the Earth and everything that's in it,
> And – which is more – you'll be a Man, my son!

☞ **ROBERT FROST** (1874–1963, American)

Probably second only to Whitman as 'great American poet'; won the Pulitzer Prize three times. His works include *Stopping by Woods on a Snowy Evening* ('And miles to go before I sleep') and *The Road Not Taken* ('Two roads diverged in a wood, and I—/I took the one less traveled by.')

☞ **W(ILLIAM) B(UTLER) YEATS** (1865–1939, Irish)
Theosophist and Rosicrucian as well as poet and playwright; dedicated his early poems to Maud Gonne. Best known are *The Song of Wandering Aengus* and *The Lake Isle of Innisfree* ('I will arise and go now, and go to Innisfree').

☞ **W(YSTAN) H(UGH) AUDEN** (1907–73, English)
Shot to renewed fame twenty years after his death thanks to the film *Four Weddings and a Funeral*. 'Stop all the clocks, cut off the telephone', which is recited at the funeral, is taken from his *Twelve Songs*.

☞ **T(HOMAS) S(TEARNS) ELIOT** (1888–1965,
      American-born, worked in England)
Author of *The Wasteland* ('April is the cruellest month') and *The Love Song of J Alfred Prufrock*.

☞ **DYLAN THOMAS** (1914–53, Welsh)
Famous drunkard, but you forgive him most things for having written *Under Milk Wood* and enabled Richard Burton to record it for posterity.

And a separate mention for the three most prominent World War I poets:

☞ SIEGFRIED SASSOON (1886–1967, English)

Yes, really – 1967. Isn't that weird? Not only did he survive the war, he went on to outlive the others by half a century. His most famous line is probably 'Everybody suddenly burst out singing.'

☞ RUPERT BROOKE (1887–1915, English)

Author of *The Old Vicarage, Grantchester*:

> *Stands the Church clock at ten to three?*
> *And is there honey still for tea?*

and of *The Soldier*:

> *If I should die, think only this of me:*
> *That there's some corner of a foreign field*
> *That is forever England.*

(And of course he did die.)

☞ WILFRED OWEN (1893–1918, English)

The one who died just a week before the armistice. Best known for *Anthem for Doomed Youth* ('What passing-bells for these who die as cattle?') and for *Dulce et decorum est,* which is actually the start of a line from Horace: 'Dulce et decorum est pro patria mori' – 'It is sweet and right to die for your country.' They were keen on that during World War I. Or at least the people who weren't in the trenches were. Owen called it 'the old lie', which seems more accurate to me.

Foreign authors

Most of us had teachers of English or General Studies who encouraged us to broaden our horizons by reading some of the foreign 'greats' in translation. Keeping this to a Top Ten has meant cheating a bit on the Greek tragedians and leaving out Horace, Ovid, Rabelais, Molière, Schiller, Balzac, Zola… and that's before I really hit the twentieth century. But I think these are the ones you are most likely to have read without knowing the original language.

~~~~~~

☞ **HOMER** (*c*.9th century BC, Greek)
The great epics the *Iliad* and the *Odyssey* are the basis of pretty much everything we know about the Trojan War and about Odysseus (Ulysses)'s ten-year journey to get home to Ithaca. Quick run-down on the Trojan War: Paris, Prince of Troy, abducted Helen, beautiful wife of Menelaus, King of Sparta (in Greece). Various Greek heroes – Odysseus, Achilles, Agamemnon – were pledged to fight to bring her back. They laid siege to Troy for ten years before finally hitting on the idea of the wooden horse: soldiers hid inside it, the Trojans were fooled into taking it within the city walls, the soldiers leapt out and the rest is history.[7] The Trojan hero was Paris's

---

7 Or not – it's probably all a complete fabrication, but you know what I mean.

elder brother, Hector. Their parents were Priam and Hecuba, and their sister Cassandra was the one who made prophecies that no one believed. Then Odysseus set off home, encountering Circe, Calypso and the Cyclops Polyphemus on the way. Back home, his wife Penelope had promised her suitors that she would marry one of them when she had finished the piece of weaving she was doing, but she secretly unravelled the day's work every night.

☞ **SOPHOCLES** (*c*.496–406 BC, Greek)

Oedipus Rex: The one about the man who accidentally married his mother. *Medea*, the one about the woman who murdered her children to avenge herself on their father (can't remember what he had done, but it must have been quite something), is by **Euripides**, who lived at much the same time. And while we're at it, there was the comic playwright **Aristophanes**, who wrote *Lysistrata*, about the women who put a stop to a war by refusing to have sex with their husbands.

☞ **VIRGIL** (70–19 BC, Roman)

The *Aeneid*, the story of the Trojan prince Aeneas, the ancestor of the Roman people (also an ancestor of Romulus and Remus, who actually founded the city). Some of the *Aeneid* is inspired by Homer and relates the fall of Troy. Escaping from Troy, Aeneas eventually reached Italy but stopped off en route in Carthage, where he had an affair with the queen, Dido, who burned herself alive when he left her. The first words of the

Aeneid are 'Arma virumque cano' – 'I sing of arms and the man' – which is where the title of Shaw's play comes from.

☞ **DANTE ALIGHIERI** (1265–1321, Italian)

The Divine Comedy, another epic, divided into three parts: *Inferno* (Hell), *Purgatoria* and *Paradiso*. It narrates Dante's journey through these three worlds, the first two guided by Virgil, the final by Beatrice, a woman with whom he had been madly in love since he was nine, although it seems they met only twice. Hell is shown as having various circles, indicating degrees of suffering, depending on how bad you had been in life: the ninth and worst contains the poets.

☞ **MIGUEL DE CERVANTES** (1547–1616, Spanish)

Don Quixote: Don Quixote is an elderly gentleman whose brain has been turned by reading too many novels of chivalry (cf. *Northanger Abbey*, p.35) and who decides to go out into the world and do noble deeds of knight errantry. To this end, he imagines that a local village girl is the glamorous lady in whose name these deeds will be carried out and christens her Dulcinea del Toboso. His steed is actually a broken-down old horse called Rosinante – which means 'previously a broken-down old horse'. He adopts Sancho Panza as his squire and goes around attacking windmills because he thinks they are giants, and similar foolishness.

☞ **JOHANN WOLFGANG VON GOETHE** (1749–1832, German)

Faust is the story of the man who sells his soul to the devil – here called Mephistopheles – in return for worldly success. Surprisingly, he is saved by angels. Christopher Marlowe's play *Doctor Faustus* was the inspiration for Goethe's work, which in turn inspired Gounod's opera *Faust* and Berlioz's *Damnation of Faust*. Marlowe's ending is the more predictable soul-in-torment one and his play contains the famous line 'Is this the face that launched a thousand ships?' referring to Helen of Troy.

☞ **VICTOR HUGO** (1802–85, French)

Notre-Dame de Paris, known to us as *The Hunchback of Notre-Dame*, and *Les Miserables*, popularly known as *The Glums*. The hunchback Quasimodo is the bell-ringer at Notre-Dame and the plot concerns his love for the gypsy girl Esmeralda. If you can watch the Charles Laughton film without weeping piteously, you are not a nice person. *Les Mis* is set in Paris in 1815, at the time of the Battle of Waterloo. The central character, Jean Valjean, is a reformed thief who is persecuted by the police agent Javert.

☞ **GUSTAV FLAUBERT** (1821–80, French)

Madame Bovary: This is the one where she closes the blinds on the carriage and has sex while driving round Rouen. There's a bit more to it than that, but that's the scene that sticks in most people's minds. Anyway, Madame Bovary – Emma – is married to a worthy but dull provincial doctor, Charles. She longs for glamour and passion and acquires (consecutively, not simultaneously) two lovers, Léon and Rodolphe. It ends in tears. And arsenic.

☞ **FYODOR DOSTOEVSKY** (1821–81, Russian)
Crime and Punishment: An impoverished student, Raskolnikov, murders a old nasty old woman pawnbroker, reasoning that in so doing he is benefiting humanity. Pretty soon his conscience starts to tell him that this may not be entirely true.

☞ **LEO TOLSTOY** (1828–1910, Russian)
Anna Karenina: Another woman married to a boring man; this one falls in love with Vronsky and throws herself under a train. The massively long *War and Peace* has a vast cast and is said to be one of the richest novels ever written, with a backdrop of Moscow and St Petersburg during the Napoleonic Wars. It concerns nice Pierre and ambitious Prince Andrei both being involved with beautiful but silly Natasha, and there must be more to it than that but (strictly between you and me) I've got a few hundred pages to go.

And just to show that Europe didn't have all the good (or indeed all the overrated) writers, here are a few...

American classics

☞ **HARRIET BEECHER STOWE** (1811–96)

Uncle Tom's Cabin: A violently anti-slavery novel (published in 1852, when this was *the* political hot potato in America), this nevertheless rejoices in the subtitle *Life Among the Lowly*. Uncle Tom is a slave who is bought by a Mr St Clare after he (Tom) has saved the life of his (Mr St Clare's) daughter, the saintly Little Eva. Like all saintly women in Victorian novels, Little Eva is also sickly and soon dies. When Mr St Clare is killed in an accident, Tom is sold to the evil Simon Legree, who eventually has him whipped to death for refusing to betray the whereabouts of two other runaway slaves. There are no shades of grey in this novel – Tom is a saint too, and Legree is a monster. But perhaps the most famous character is the slave girl Topsy – the one who didn't know where she came from (i.e. didn't realize that God had made her – it's that sort of book) and said, 'I s'pect I growed.'

☞ **MARK TWAIN** (Samuel Langhorne Clemens, 1835–1910)

The Adventures of Tom Sawyer and *The Adventures of Huckleberry Finn*: Tom is brought up by his respectable Aunt Polly; his friend Huck seems to have no family and leads (to Tom's mind) a much more interesting life. Their adventures include accidentally witnessing a murder committed by Injun Joe (you don't find many characters with names like that these days, do you?), turning up alive and well at their own funerals and preventing an innocent man being convicted of Joe's crime. But the most famous episode is the one where Tom, forced to whitewash Aunt Polly's fence as a punishment, cons his friends into doing the work for him by persuading them that it is a privilege.

That's all in *Tom Sawyer*. *Huck Finn*, with the issue of slavery at its heart, is a much more serious book. It is also harder work because it is narrated by Huck in Missouri dialect. Huck is kidnapped by his father, who does exist after all and who hopes to get hold of the money the boys found in Injun Joe's cave. Huck escapes by faking his own death and runs away with a slave, Jim, who is then suspected of Huck's murder. Once everything is sorted, Huck has the opportunity to make a home with Tom's Aunt Sally [sic – he has more than one aunt] but runs away rather than submit to being 'sivilized'.

☞ J(EROME) D(AVID) SALINGER (1919–)
The Catcher in the Rye: The ultimate disaffected-teenager novel, told in the first person by sixteen-year-old Holden Caulfield, who loathes everything to do with his life and his parents' 'phony' middle-class values. He runs away to New York, gets involved with drink and prostitutes but is ultimately redeemed by the love of a good woman – in this case his sister Phoebe. (Not *that* sort of love.)

☞ JOHN STEINBECK (1920–68)

The Grapes of Wrath: After the Oklahoma dustbowl disaster of the 1930s, the Joad family – and other farmers – abandon their land and head for what they imagine is a Promised Land in California, only to find that life is no easier there. In the course of a strike, Tom Joad (Henry Fonda in the film) kills a man to avenge the death of his friend Jim Casy and is forced to leave his family to struggle on without him. The title comes from *The Battle Hymn of the Republic* – 'He is trampling out the vintage where the grapes of wrath are stored.'

☞ JOSEPH HELLER (1923–99)

Catch-22: Too recent to have been taught when I was at school but a 'classic' now, and one of the few novels whose title has *created* an idiom rather than employing an existing quotation. The plot centres on a group of American fighter pilots in Italy during World War II and their efforts to avoid flying suicidal missions. The problem is that the only way they can get out of flying missions is if they are crazy – but the moment they ask to be grounded because flying the missions is crazy, they are deemed to be entirely sane, and therefore fit to fly.

Yossarian was moved very deeply by the absolute simplicity of this clause...

'That's some catch, that Catch-22,' he observed.

'It's the best there is,' Doc Daneeka agreed.

☞ HARPER LEE (1926–)

To Kill a Mockingbird: The story of a white lawyer in a Deep South town who defends a black man, Tom Robinson, wrongly accused of raping a white girl. The lawyer (played by Gregory Peck in the film) rejoices in the name of Atticus Finch and the book is written in the first person, the narrator being Atticus's young daughter Scout. This is the only novel Harper Lee (who is a woman, by the way) has ever published.

MATHS

I did maths up to what is now GCSE stage and we called it maths. If you carried on beyond that, it became much more complicated and you started calling it mathematics. At my level, it was divided into **arithmetic, algebra, geometry** and **trigonometry**, in ascending order of incomprehensibility, and I've taken aspects of those four subjects here. If you went far enough to get into calculus, you've probably forgotten even more about it than I have.

Arithmetic

Arithmetic is sums – adding, subtracting, multiplying and dividing – but even it comes with its own vocabulary:

- If you add two or more numbers together, their total is a **sum**. So 7 is the sum of 4+3.
- With subtraction, you find the **difference** between two numbers: the difference between 9 and 7 is the smaller number subtracted from the larger, 9–7, and the difference is 2.
- If you multiply two or more numbers together, the answer is a **product**. So 30 is the product of 6x5.
- With division, you divide a **divisor** into a **dividend**

and the answer is a **quotient**. If the sum doesn't work out exactly, the bit left over is called a **remainder**. So 15 divided by 2 gives a quotient of 7 with a remainder of 1.

☞ LONG MULTIPLICATION

If, like me, you are old enough to have done maths exams without the aid of a calculator, you will have learned the times tables. The best one is the 11 times table because it goes 11, 22, 33, 44, etc – but all goes a bit wrong after 99. We learned by rote up to 12x12 = 144; beyond that you needed to understand what you were doing. For example:

$$\begin{array}{r} 147 \\ \times\ 63 \\ \hline \end{array}$$

Our way of writing numbers doesn't go higher than 9, so when you get to 10 you have to use two digits. The right-hand digit in any whole number represents the units; to the left are the tens and then the hundreds and so on. So 63 is made up of 3 units plus 6 tens, or 60. And in this sum you need to multiply 147 by each of those elements separately.

Start from the right: 3x7 = 21, so you write down the 1 and 'carry' 2 to the next column.

3x4 = 12, plus the 2 you have carried = 14. Write down the 4 and carry 1.

3x1 = 3, plus the 1 you have carried= 4.

So 3x147 = 441.

To multiply 147 by 60, put a 0 in the right hand column and multiply by 6 (because any number multiplied by 10 or a multiple of 10 ends in 0).

6x7 = 42, so write down the 2 and carry 4.

6x4 = 24, plus the 4 you have carried = 28. Write down the 8 and carry 2.

6x1 = 6, plus the 2 you have carried = 8.

So 60x147 = 8820.

63x147 is therefore the sum of 60x147 (8820) and 3x147 (441), which equals 9261.

Or

$$\begin{array}{r} 147 \\ \times\ 63 \\ \hline 441 \\ 8820 \\ \hline 9261 \end{array}$$

If you remember Tom Lehrer's song about the New Math, you'll know that he went on to do his sum in base 8, but I think we might skip over that.

☞ LONG DIVISION

Division is multiplication in reverse, so let's start with 9261 and divide it by 63. (With luck, we'll end up with 147.)

If you have a divisor of 12 or less, the times tables does (or did) the work for you: you *know* (or knew) that 72 divided by 8 was 9, without having to work it out. But with a number larger than 12, you have to be more scientific:

$$63\overline{)\ 9261}$$

With division, you work through the number from left to right.

You can't divide 63 into 9, for the simple reason that 63 is bigger than 9. So look at the next column. You *can* divide 63 into 92 – once, so you write a 1 at the top of the sum. But it doesn't go into 92 once exactly – there is a remainder, which is the difference between 92 and 63: in other words 92–63, which is 29.

Carry 29 forward into the next column and put it in front of the 6, to give 296. Does 63 go into 296? Yes, it must do, because 296 is bigger than 63, but how many times? Well, look at the left-hand figures of the two numbers, and you'll see something that you can solve using the times table: 6 into 29. That's easy: four 6's are 24, so 6 goes into 29 four times, with a bit left over. So it's likely that 63 will go into 296 four times with a bit left over. Indeed 4x63 = 252, and the bit left over is 296–252 = 44.

Write 4 at the top of the sum, next to the 1, and carry 44 forward into the next column to make 441. How many times does 63 go into 441? Well, 6 goes into 44 seven times (6x7 = 42), so let's try that. And, conveniently, 63x7 = 441. Which means that 63 goes into 441 exactly seven times, with nothing left over, and you have the answer to your sum: 147. Aha!

Fractions, decimals and percentages

☞ PROPER FRACTIONS

A **fraction** is technically any form of number that is not a whole number; what most of us think of as fractions – numbers such as ½, ⅔, ¾, etc – are properly called vulgar, simple or common fractions (as opposed to decimal fractions, see below).

The top number in these fractions is called the **numerator**, the bottom one the **denominator**.

In fact, the examples given above are all **proper** fractions, with the numerator smaller than the denominator (i.e. the fraction represents less than 1). In an **improper** fraction, the reverse is true, as in $^{22}/_7$ (an approximation for pi, see p.76), which can also be written as $3^1/_7$, because 7 goes into 22 three times, with a remainder of 1.

If you want to do sums involving fractions, it is important to know that if you divide or multiply both numerator and denominator by the same number, you produce a fraction that is the same value as the original fraction. Take ½. Multiply both numerator and denominator by 2 and you get $^2/_4$. Which is still a half, because 2 is half of 4. Or multiply ½ by 3 and you get $^3/_6$. Which, again, is still a half, because 3 is half of 6.

The same principle applies to division: if you start with $^3/_6$ and divide top and bottom by 3, you reduce your fraction down to ½ again. This is called 'cancelling by three'. When you can't cancel any more, the fraction is 'in its lowest terms'.

With addition and subtraction, however, you can only add and subtract fractions that have the same denominator. You can add ½+½ and get $^2/_2$ – which equals 1. Obvious, really – two halves make a whole. But what you have done is add the two numerators together. The denominator stays the same, because you are adding like to like. (It's no different from adding 1 apple to 1 apple to get 2 apples.)

Now say you want to add ½+⅓. The lowest common denominator of 2 and 3 (the smallest number into which both will divide) is 6. To turn ½ into sixths, you need to multiply both parts of the fraction by 3:

$$\frac{1 \times 3}{2 \times 3} = \frac{3}{6}$$

So ½ is the same thing as $^3/_6$.

To convert $^1/_3$ into sixths, you need to multiply both parts by 2:

$$\frac{1 \times 2 = 2}{3 \times 2 = 6}$$

So $^1/_3$ is the same thing as $^2/_6$.

Now you have something that you can add, on the same principle of adding the numerators together:

$$^3/_6 + \,^2/_6 = \,^5/_6$$

The same applies to subtraction.

$$^7/_{10} - ^3/_{10} = \,^4/_{10}.$$

But both 4 and 10 can be divided by 2, to give the simpler fraction $^2/_5$.

☞ **DECIMAL FRACTIONS**

The word decimal means *to do with ten* and our numerical system is based on multiples of ten. As I said when talking about multiplication, a single-digit number – say 6 – means that you have six units of whatever it is. When you have more than nine, you have to use two digits, with the one representing the tens on the left and the one representing the units on the right.

Decimal fractions work on the same principle, except that they go from right to left. The fraction is separated from the whole number by a dot called a **decimal point**. The figure immediately to the right of it represents tenths, to the right of that is hundredths and so on. So 1.1 (pronounced one point one) = 1 plus one tenth of 1; 1.2 = $1+^2/_{10}$ (or $^1/_5$, see above); 1.25 (pronounced one point two five) = $1+^2/_{10}+^5/_{100}$, or $1+^{25}/_{100}$.

1.25 is an interesting example, because it is the same as 1¼. How do we know that? Well, let's go back to the idea of dividing numerators and denominators by the same thing. $^{25}/_{100}$ can be divided by 5 to give $^5/_{20}$. But 5 and 20 are both also divisible by 5, giving ¼. (Once you've got your numerator down to 1, you know that you have simplified the fraction as far as it will go.) So 1.25 is exactly the same as 1¼.

Decimal fractions that are less than 1 can be written either 0.25 or just .25 – it's the same thing.

☞ **RECURRING DECIMALS**
Not everything divides neatly into tens, so sometimes a decimal fraction can be no more than an approximation. $^1/_3$, for example, is 0.333 recurring – no matter how many threes you add, you will never get a decimal that is exactly equal to one third.

If a decimal recurs, you can be certain that it's the same as some vulgar fraction, e.g. 0.222 recurring is $^2/_9$, 0.142857142857142857 recurring is $^1/_7$. A recurring decimal is sometimes indicated with a dot above the last digit, which is sort of the equivalent of '…' or 'etc etc etc'.

Pi is different (see p.76). Its decimal expansion goes on for ever but without recurring, because it isn't the same as any vulgar fraction. Pi is called a **transcendental** number and it's probably the only one you'll ever meet.

☞ **PERCENTAGES**

Per cent means *by a hundred*, so anything expressed as a percentage is a fraction (or part, if you prefer) of 100. So 25% is twenty-five parts of a hundred, or $^{25}/_{100}$ or 0.25. If you've been paying attention, you'll know that that is the same as a quarter.

Similarly, 50% is $^{50}/_{100}$, which can be cancelled down to $^{25}/_{50}$, which is $^{5}/_{10}$, which is ½.

Mean, median and mode

In arithmetical terms, **mean** is simply a posh word for **average**. (Interesting that the posh word is four letters and one syllable, whereas the day-to-day one is seven letters and three syllables, but this is a chapter on maths, so let's not get sidetracked.)

You calculate a mean by adding a group of numbers together and dividing by the number of numbers. (Strictly speaking, this is the **arithmetic mean** – there are some other sorts of mean too, but only mathematicians are interested in them.)

So the mean of 4, 8, 12 and 16 is the total of the four numbers, divided by 4:

$$4+8+12+16 = 40, \text{ divided by } 4 = 10$$

And it works for any number of numbers: let's say that a class of eleven children gets the following marks in an exam: 55, 57, 57, 65, 66, 69, 70, 72, 75, 79, 83. The total of the marks is 748 (take my word for it, I did it on the computer); divide that by 11 and you get a mean of 68.

The **median** of a set of values is literally the middle one. In the set of marks above, it is 69. There are five marks lower than 69, and five marks higher than 69 – never mind their actual values. The median of an even number of values is the average of the middle two, e.g. the median of 1, 4, 9, 16, 25, 36 is 12.5 – half-way between 9 and 16.

The **mode** of a set of values is the most common value. The mode of our set of marks is 57, because it is the only one that occurs more than once.

Measurements

The metric and imperial systems are two different sets of units used to measure the same things. Just as Fahrenheit and Celsius both measure temperature, but in different ways (see p.100), so the metric and imperial systems quantify length, weight and all sorts of other things, using different units.

Metric units are also sometimes called SI units, which stands for Système Internationale, and even though there isn't a chapter on French in this book I'm not going to insult your intelligence by translating that.

The metric system calculates in tens or multiples of tens. The imperial system doesn't, and to the uninitiated it can seem pretty random. (The pro-imperial way of looking at this is that imperial units all used to mean something sensible, e.g. the foot was the length of a man's foot; the yard was the distance from his nose to the tip of his outstretched arm, etc. By contrast, the metric system slavishly uses the number 10 as a multiplier, and if the units it produces bear no relation to real life, that's just tough.)

☞ LENGTH

The basic unit of length in the metric system is the metre, with subdivisions and multiples for measuring little things and big things. Most commonly used are the millimetre (a thousandth of a metre), the centimetre (a hundredth of a metre, or ten. millimetres), and the kilometre (a thousand metres).

In imperial, length is measured in inches, feet, yards and miles, and occasionally also in chains and furlongs. There are 12 inches in a foot, 3 feet (36 inches) in a yard, 22 yards in a chain, 10 chains in a furlong, and 8 furlongs (1760 yards, 5280 feet) in a mile. Other units are still in use for some special purposes, e.g. the fathom (6 feet) for measuring the depth of the sea, and the hand (4 inches) for measuring the height of a horse.

To convert between the two:

✒ 1 inch = 2.54 centimetres, so to convert inches to centimetres, multiply by 2.54. To convert centimetres to inches, divide by 2.54. Remember that a centimetre is shorter than an inch, so you should have a larger number of centimetres.

✒ 1 yard = 0.91 metres; 1 metre = 1.09 yards or 3.3 feet. Yards and feet are shorter than metres, so you will have a larger number of them.

✒ 1 mile = 1.6 kilometres; 1 kilometre = 0.625 ($^5/_8$) of a mile. This time the metric unit is smaller, so you have more kilometres than miles.

✒ A nautical mile (and you'll never guess where that is used) is about 1.15 miles, or *exactly* 1852 metres.

☞ WEIGHT

In metric, weight is measured in grams or kilograms. (You can have milligrams and centigrams, but a gram is already pretty small, so unless you're a pharmacist or something of that sort you don't often need them.) A kilogram is a thousand grams.

In imperial it is ounces, pounds, stones, hundredweights and tons: 16 ounces (oz) = 1 pound (lb, from *libra*, the Latin for pound); 14 pounds = 1 stone; 8 stone (112 lb) = 1 hundred-weight (cwt); 20 hundredweight (2240 lb) = 1 ton. This is sometimes called a long ton, because the North Americans use a short ton of 2000 lb. Also they don't use stones. Actually nobody uses hundredweight much any more, either.

✎ 1 gram (or g or gm) = about $^1/_{28}$ ounce, so to convert grams to ounces, divide by 28. To convert ounces to grams, multiply by 28.

✎ 1 kilogram (or kilo or kg) is about 2.2 pounds, so multiply kilograms by 2.2, divide pounds by 2.2.

✎ A metric tonne (always spelled thus) is 1000 kilograms, or 2205 pounds, just a bit smaller than an imperial ton.

☞ CAPACITY

In metric, this is measured in litres; in imperial in fluid ounces, pints, quarts and gallons. Made a bit more complicated by the fact that the imperial units differ between the UK and the US.

In the UK, 20 fluid ounces make a pint, 2 pints make a quart and there are 4 quarts (8 pints) in a gallon. A litre is about 1.75 pints, so to convert pints to litres, divide by 1.75; to convert litres to pints, multiply by 1.75 (pints are smaller, so you will have more of them).

In the US, 16 fluid ounces make a pint, so the US pint and gallon are smaller than the UK ones. To convert US pints to litres, divide by 2.1.

Algebra and equations

Algebra is the branch of maths that uses symbols (normally letters of the alphabet) to represent unknown numbers, along the lines of $a+b = 5$. If you assign a value to a, you can calculate b: if $a = 2$ then $b = 3$. This is known as an **algebraic equation**.

The main thing to remember when solving equations is that one side of the '=' sign is equal to the other side, so anything that you do to one side, you need to do to the other.[8]

For example, to solve the equation

$$3a+1 = 16-2a$$

you first add $2a$ to each side, giving

$$5a+1 = 16$$

Then subtract 1 from each side, giving

$$5a = 15$$

---

8 You're allowed to do almost anything to an equation, as long as you do the same thing to both sides of it. You are not allowed, however, to a) take square roots; or b) divide by 0. You wouldn't normally divide anything by 0 anyway, but if you were to divide something by, say, $a-3$ and it turned out that a equalled 3, you'd get some very odd answers. We'll come back to square roots later in this section.

Now you can divide both sides by 5 and announce proudly that $a = 3$.

☞ **SIMULTANEOUS EQUATIONS**

A more complicated form of algebraic equation, in which you have two or more unknowns. The general rule is that you must have exactly the same number of equations as you have unknowns in order to find the value of each. If you have fewer equations, there will be lots of solutions and no way to choose between them. If you have too many equations, there will no solution at all.

This assumes that the equations are all different and don't contradict each other. For example,

$$a+h = 6$$
$$2a+2b = 12$$

are no good as a pair of simultaneous equations, because they both say exactly the same thing, while

$$a+b = 6$$
$$a+b = 7$$

don't work either, because there's no way both of them can be true at the same time.

Let's look at a better-behaved set of simultaneous equations:

$$a+b = 6$$
$$a-b = 2$$

One way of solving these is to add the two equations together, so:

$$a+a+b-b = 6+2$$

or, more simply, $2a = 8$ (because the $+b$ and $-b$ cancel each other out).

From there you can calculate that $a = 4$ and, because $a+b = 6$, b must equal 2. Which is verified by the second equation, $4-2 = 2$.

The principle remains the same however many unknowns you have:

$$a+b+c = 24$$
$$a+b-c = 16$$
$$2a+b = 32$$

Add the first two equations together and you get $2a+2b = 40$ (because this time the c's cancel each other out).

Now look at the third equation. It's quite similar to the sum of the first two. Subtract one from the other:

$$2a+2b-2a-b = 40-32$$

The a's cancel each other out, so $2b-b$ (in other words, b) = 8.

Go back to the third equation, which contains only a's and b's, and substitute 8 for b:

$$2a+8 = 32$$

Deduct 8 from each side of the equation to give

$$2a = 32-8 = 24$$

which means that a = 12.

Now go back to the first equation and substitute both a and b:

$$12+8+c = 24$$
$$20+c = 24$$
$$c = 24-20 = 4$$

Verify this by going to the second equation:

$$12[a]+8[b]-c[4] = 16$$

which is true.

☞ QUADRATIC EQUATIONS

These are more complex again, because they involve a square – that is, a number multiplied by itself and written with a raised ^{2} after it – so 16 is 4^2 and 36 is 6^2. Thus 4 is the square root of

16 and 6 the square root of 36. The symbol for a **square root** is √. Actually, $(-4)^2$ is also 16, so 16 has two square roots, +4 and –4. Any positive number has two square roots. A negative number doesn't have any square roots at all, because if you multiply a negative by a negative you get a positive.

An algebraic expression can also be a square: the square of $a+4$ is $(a+4)$x$(a+4)$. You do this by multiplying each of the elements in the first bracket by each of the elements in the second:

$$(a \times a) + (a \times 4) + (4 \times a) + (4 \times 4)$$
$$= a^2 + 8a + 16$$

To solve a quadratic equation, you need to turn both sides of it into a perfect square, which is easier to explain if we look at an example:

$$a^2 + 8a = 48$$

The rule for 'completing the square' in order to solve a quadratic equation is 'take the number before the a, square it and divide by 4' (don't ask – it just is). 8 squared (64) divided by 4 is 16, so we add that to both sides; reassuringly we already know that adding 16 to this equation will create a perfect square, because we just did it, in the previous equation.

$$a^2 + 8a + 16 = 48 + 16 = 64$$

Taking the square root of each side gives:

$a+4 = 8$ (because 8 is the square root of 64)

Again, we know that $a+4$ is the square root of $a^2+8a+16$, because it was part of the sum we did on the previous page. Anyway, we now have a simple sum to establish that $a = 4$.

Wait a minute, though... taking the square root of both sides of an equation is something we're not allowed to do. Why is this? Because a positive number like 64 has *two* square roots, +8 and −8. So the truth of the matter is that actually

$$a+4 = +8 \text{ or } -8$$

so a equals either +4 or −12.

That was easy because I chose the numbers so that it would be, but the beauty of algebra is that the same principle applies whatever the numbers involved.

So if your equation is

$$a^2+12a+14 = 33$$

you first simplify the equation by getting rid of the 14. Subtract it from both sides to leave

$$a^2+12a = 33-14 = 19$$

Square the 12 to give 144, divide by 4 to give 36 and – as always – add that to both sides:

$$a^2+12a+36 = 19+36 = 55$$

The square root of that gives you

$$a+6 = \sqrt{55} = \text{(approximately)} \ 7.4, \ or, \\ of \ course \ -7.4$$

Deduct 6 from each side to leave the simple statement $a = 1.4$ or −13.4.

You can check that this is right by going back to the original equation and putting in $a = 1.4$:

$$a^2+12a+14 = 33$$

becomes

$$(1.4 \times 1.4)+(12 \times 1.4)+14 = 1.96+16.8+14 =$$

(near enough for the purposes of this exercise)

$$2+17+14 = 33.$$

QED, as they say. You'll find it also works out with $a = -13.4$.

Geometry

Geometry is about measuring lines and angles and assessing the relationship between them, so let's start with some ways of measuring.

✎ The **perimeter** of a two-dimensional object is the total length of all its sides. If these sides are straight, it's a matter of simple addition: a rectangle measuring 4cm by 5cm has two sides 4cm long and two sides 5cm long, so its perimeter is 4+5+4+5 = 18cm.

✎ The **area** of a four-sided figure is calculated by multiplying the length by the breadth: in the above example 4x5 = 20 square centimetres (cm^2).

✎ **Volume** is calculated in the same way, by multiplying the length by the breadth by the height (or, if you prefer, the area by the height). So, a box whose base measures 4cm by 5cm and which is 6cm high has a volume of 4x5x6 = 120 cubed centimetres (cm^3).

The volume of a pyramid is the area of the base multiplied by the height, divided by 3:

$$\frac{h \times b}{3}$$

It's when you get to circles that it all becomes more complicated, because then you have to start dealing with…

☞ **PI**

Pi (π) is the Greek equivalent of the Roman *p* and is used in maths to represent the ratio of the circumference of a circle to its diameter. Depending on how sophisticated you are as a mathematician, you can say that π = 3.142, 3.14159 or 3.14159265358979323846264338332795, but even then it is not a hundred per cent exact (somebody has calculated it to two billion decimal places, but they should clearly get out more). Expressed as a fraction, pi is roughly $3^1/_7$ or $^{22}/_7$.

Before we go on, three more quick definitions:

✔ the **circumference** of a circle is its perimeter, the distance round the outside.
✔ the **diameter** is the length of a straight line through the middle, from one point on the circumference to another.
✔ the **radius** is half the diameter; that is, the distance from the centre of the circle to the circumference.

So, to calculate the circumference of a circle, you multiply the diameter by π: a circle 7cm in diameter has a circumference of $7 \times ^{22}/_7$ = approximately 22cm. The formula for this can be expressed as πd, but is more usually given as $2(\pi r)$.

Area is πr^2, that is, π times the radius squared. So a circle of 6cm radius has an area of $^{22}/_7 \times (6 \times 6)$ = approximately 113cm^2.

The three-dimensional equivalent to a circle is a **sphere**, and its volume is calculated by the formula $^4/_3\pi r^3$ – that is four-thirds (or one and one-third) of the product of π and the radius cubed (multiplied by itself and then by itself again). So a sphere with a radius of 6cm has a volume of $^4/_3$xπx(6x6x6) = approximately 905cm^3.

A **cone** is effectively a pyramid with a circular base, so the pyramid formula applies: a cone with a base 6cm in diameter and a height of 10cm has a base area of πx(6x6) = approximately 113cm^2, and a volume of:

$$\frac{10x113}{3}$$

or

$$\frac{1130}{3}$$

which equals approximately 377cm^3.

☞ **TRIANGLES**

The area of a triangle is calculated by:

$$\frac{base \times height}{2}$$

There are three types of triangle, depending on the length of their sides:

✒ an **equilateral** triangle has three sides of equal length.

✒ an **isosceles** triangle has two sides of equal length.

✒ a **scalene** triangle has three sides that are all of different lengths.

The sum total of the angles of a triangle, whatever its shape, is 180°. A **right angle** is 90°; any angle smaller than 90° is called an **acute angle**, while anything above 90° but lower than 180° is **obtuse**. In a right-angled triangle, the side opposite the right angle (also always the longest side), is called the **hypotenuse**, which brings us neatly to...

☞ PYTHAGORAS'S THEOREM

This states that the square on the hypotenuse is equal to the sum of the squares on the other two sides. The simplest example of this is what is called a 3:4:5 triangle, in which the hypotenuse is 5cm (or inches or miles, it doesn't matter) and the other two sides are 3cm and 4cm.

The square on the side that is 3cm long is 9cm² (3x3), the square on the 4cm side is 16cm² (4x4), and when you add them together you get 25cm², which is the square on the hypotenuse (5x5).

This can also be remembered using the formula $a^2+b^2 = c^2$, where c is the hypotenuse.

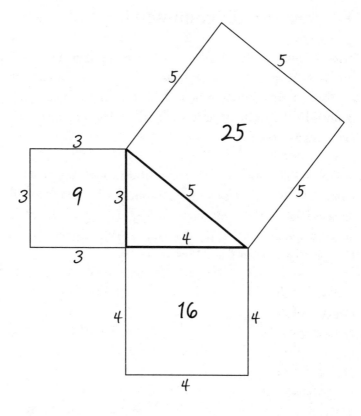

The burning question, of course, is why does it matter? Well, it *could* have had some practical value in the ancient world. It has been suggested, for example, that the Egyptians could have used ropes in the proportion 3:4:5 to produce right angles when building the pyramids. Unfortunately there isn't the remotest scrap of evidence that they did any such thing. In fact, Pythagoras's theorem matters most to mathematicians, because it is fundamental to our next topic.

Trigonometry

Trigonometry is 'the branch of mathematics that deals with the relations between the sides and angles of a triangle', and a **trigonometric function** is 'any function of an angle that is defined by the relationship between the sides and angles of a right-angled triangle'.

There are six basic trigonometric functions: sine, cosine, tangent, cotangent, secant and cosecant, and they are calculated as follows. In a right-angled triangle where the other two angles are valued at x and y degrees, the side opposite x is a, the side opposite y is b and the hypotenuse is c:

$\sin x = a/c$
$\cos x = b/c$
$\tan x = a/b$
$\cot x = b/a$
$\sec x = c/b$
$\csc x = c/a$

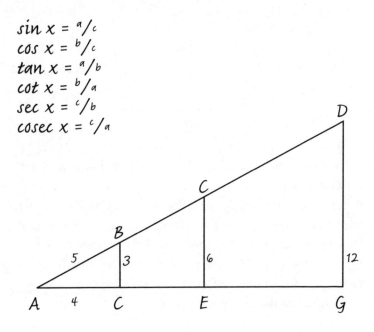

Why do we care? Well, the point is that the functions or ratios remain the same whatever the size of the triangle. So if you know the sine of a 45° angle in a triangle whose sides measure 3, 4 and 5cm, you can extrapolate all sorts of measurements for a much larger triangle with the same proportions.

The trigonometric version of Pythagoras's theorem tells us that, for any angle x,

$$sin^2x + cos^2x = 1$$

where sin^2x is a conventional way of writing $(sin x)^2$ without the need for brackets. If you know the sine of an angle, you can use this formula to calculate all the rest of the trigonometric functions given above.

Trigonometry is vital to the study of higher mathematics and the sciences. At a more comprehensible and practical level, it is used in surveying, map-making, engineering, astronomy, navigation and so on, for example to calculate the height of trees and mountains. Hugh Grant used it in *The Englishman Who Went Up a Hill But Came Down a Mountain,* so it must be true.

SCIENCE

At school this was divided into **biology**, **chemistry** and **physics**, as if there were no other sciences to consider, which is why I have put the bit about the solar system (which might be considered astronomy) in the General Studies chapter of this book. I also at one stage studied physicswithchemistry as one subject, so if you take issue with any of the subdivisions towards the end of this chapter, that's why.

Biology

From the Greek *study of life*, so this is all the stuff about plants and animals and how the human body works.

☞ PHOTOSYNTHESIS

This is the process by which plants convert carbon dioxide and water into the carbohydrates they need for growth, using energy that they absorb from light (hence the *photo* element). Light is absorbed into the plant by the green pigment called **chlorophyll**, stored mainly in the leaves, which provides the green colour of so many plants. In fact plants need only the hydrogen element from water (H_2O), so photosynthesis releases oxygen back into the atmosphere, helping the rest of us to breathe.

☞ THE STRUCTURE OF A PLANT

The **flower** contains the plant's reproductive organs. The stigma, style and ovary make up the carpel, which contains the female cells; if a flower has more than one carpel these combine to form the pistil. The male organ is called the stamen and consists of an anther that contains the pollen sacs and is supported on a filament. Most plants self-pollinate, but some, such as certain hollies and the kiwi fruit, require a male and female plant of the same species in order to reproduce.

The **leaves** enable the plant to feed and breathe. They contain the chlorophyll that is essential to photosynthesis, as it absorbs light; they also contain pores (stomata) through which gases and water are absorbed and released back into the atmosphere. The shape of the leaf reflects the plant's needs: big, broad leaves are designed to absorb maximum light; the fleshy, succulent leaves of a cactus store water in case of drought.

The **stem** is the plant's support and the conduit between roots, leaves and plants. It contains phloem, a tissue that transports food round the plant, and xylem, which principally transports water. It is the xylem which hardens up to form the trunks of trees and shrubs.

The **roots** anchor the plant in the ground and absorb nutrients and water from the soil. A tap root system has a single main root; a fibrous system has – well, lots of fibres. In root vegetables such as turnips and carrots, the vegetable part is in fact a swollen root. Adventitious roots are less common; the name means *coming from the outside* and these roots grow in unusual places, such as from the stem.

☞ THE CARBON CYCLE

The process by which carbon (in the form of carbon dioxide) is absorbed from the atmosphere during photosynthesis, transferred from one organism to another and eventually released back into the atmosphere is known as the carbon cycle. For example, a plant takes in carbon dioxide; the plant is eaten by a herbivorous animal, which is in turn eaten by a carnivore; when the animal dies, its rotting body releases carbon dioxide. Alternatively, the herbivorous animal excretes its waste, which also degrades to give off carbon dioxide.

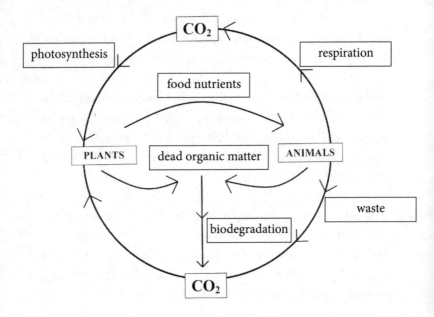

Which is a nice link from plants to the human body.

☞ CHROMOSOMES

A normal human body has forty-six chromosomes, made up of twenty-two matched pairs and two sex chromosomes. Half of each pair, and a single sex chromosome, are found in the sperm, the other half in the egg – fusion of the two creates the human embryo. Sex chromosomes are of two types, called X (female) and Y (male). The egg always contains an X chromosome, so the sex of the embryo is determined by whether a sperm is carrying an X or Y chromosome. Other chromosomes dictate other genetic factors such as hair and eye colour.

Chromosomes are made up of DNA, RNA and protein.

DNA stands for deoxyribonucleic acid and is fundamental to the organization and functioning of living cells. It consists of the famous 'double helix' (identified by the scientists Crick and Watson in 1953), with two strands coiled around each other. When the strands of a helix separate, each provides a template for the synthesis of an identical strand, containing the same genetic information. This enables normal growth, cell repair and the production of cells that will turn into the next generation – which is why we produce human babies rather than tiger cubs, and why tigers produce tiger cubs rather than roses.

RNA stands for ribonucleic acid, which occurs as a single strand and contains different sugars and bases, but is otherwise structurally similar to DNA. It's vital to the synthesis of…

Proteins, which fulfil many important roles in a living organism – they are involved in the make-up of tissue, the properties of muscles and the functioning of hormones, the immune system and the digestive system, to name but a few. They are manufactured within cells using information conveyed by the DNA and RNA.

☞ BONES OF THE HUMAN BODY

The human skeleton is made up of over two hundred bones, held together by fibrous tissue called **ligaments**, and linked at the **joints**. Joints allow varying degrees of movement from none (between the bones which make up the skull) through quite a bit (the hinge joints at the elbow and knee) to lots (the ball-and-socket joints at the hip and shoulder).

The principal bones of the body, starting at the top and working down are:

- **cranium:** skull
- **spine:** made up of twenty-six smaller bones called vertebrae
- **clavicle:** collar bone
- **scapula:** shoulder blade
- **humerus:** upper arm
- **radius** and **ulna:** lower arm – the radius is the broader one on the thumb side, the ulna the narrower one on the little finger side
- **carpus:** a collective name for the bones of the wrist, individually known as carpals

- **metacarpus:** ditto for the five long bones of the hand
- **phalanges:** fingers
- **sacrum:** actually a fusion of five vertebrae attached to the **hip bone**
- **coccyx:** tail bone, a fusion of the lowest four vertebrae
- **femur:** thigh bone
- **patella:** knee cap
- **tibia** and **fibula:** lower leg – the tibia is the broader one that runs down towards the big toe, the fibula the narrower one that runs towards the little toe
- **tarsus:** a collective name for the bones of the ankle and heel, individually known as tarsals
- **metatarsus:** ditto for the five long bones of the foot
- more **phalanges:** toes

☞ CIRCULATION OF THE BLOOD

Blood is the body's transportation system   everything from oxygen to hormones is transported round the body in the bloodstream, and its waste products, from carbon dioxide to urea, are carried away for disposal.

In order for blood to do its stuff, it needs to be pumped around, and that is the primary purpose of the **heart**. The heart is basically two pumps, each consisting of two chambers – an auricle and a ventricle – with a valve in between. The left side of the heart receives oxygen-rich blood from the lungs and forces it round the body; the right side receives the oxygen-depleted blood and returns it to the lungs to be re-oxygenated. (Oxygen, of course, comes into the lungs in the air that we breathe, and without it the cells in the body would die.)

All this requires a well-organized system of blood vessels. These are divided into **arteries**, which are strong and muscular and carry fast-flowing blood *away* from the heart, and **veins**, which are weaker and more sluggish and bring it back. The principal artery, the **aorta**, divides into smaller arteries and arterioles. Smaller veins are called venules and really tiny blood vessels, whether veins or arteries, are called capillaries.

There is, inevitably, an exception to the arteries-carry-oxygen-rich-blood rule: the pulmonary artery carries deoxygenated blood from the heart to the lungs, where it is reoxygenated and returned to to the heart via pulmonary veins. So, if you like, the pulmonery artery carries 'venous' blood.

Blood has four major components:

- **red blood cells**, which carry haemoglobin, made up of haem (an iron-containing pigment) and globin (a protein). This combines with oxygen to form oxyhaemoglobin, the means by which oxygen is transported round the body. Oxyhaemoglobin also gives the blood its red colour, which is why arterial blood is bright red whereas venous blood, having deposited oxygen in cells all over the body, has a bluish tinge.
- **white bloods cells**, or leucocytes, which fight infection.
- **platelets**, which are necessary to the clotting process.
- **plasma**, the liquid that makes the blood, well, liquid.

☞ THE DIGESTIVE SYSTEM

The digestive process is divided into four parts:

- **Ingestion**: eating food
- **Digestion**: breaking the food down into constituent parts
- **Absorption**: extracting nutrients from the food
- **Elimination**: disposing of waste

Once we swallow food or drink, it enters the **oesophagus** or gullet and passes (through a process of muscular contraction called **peristalsis**) into the stomach. From there it continues into the **small intestine** (comprising the duodenum, jejunum and ileum), where digested food is absorbed into the bloodstream. The whole process is helped by the secretion of **enzymes**. One of the effects of the digestion of protein (which we take in in the form of meat, fish, eggs, etc) is the release of **amino acids**, which are the 'building blocks' of the protein the body needs for all sorts of different purposes (see *DNA*, p.85).

Anything undigested after this stage passes into the **colon** (the beginning of the large intestine), where water is extracted from it; what remains are the faeces, which pass through the rectum and out of the body via the anus.

Organs encountered along the way include:

- the **liver**, which, in adult life, we may think of as being the one that copes with our alcohol intake, but which has many more functions to do with digestion and keeping the blood healthy.

- the **gall bladder**, which stores bile, needed in the digestion of fats.
- the **pancreas**, which secretes various enzymes and the hormones insulin and glucagon, which regulate levels of blood sugar.
- the **kidneys**, which control the amount of salt and water in the blood. Excess fluid containing waste products is filtered through the kidneys down to the bladder and leaves the body in the form of urine.

☞ THE RESPIRATORY SYSTEM

Air passes into the body via the **trachea** or wind pipe. With the help of contractions from the **diaphragm**, which is a large muscle extending across the bottom of the ribcage, it is carried down into the lungs via two smaller tubes called **bronchi**, which then split into even smaller bronchioles. Inside the lungs are lots of little air sacs or **alveoli**. Within the alveoli, oxygen is extracted from the air, absorbed into the bloodstream and carried off to the heart via the pulmonary artery (see *Circulation of the blood*, p.87). The pulmonary vein brings 'used' blood back to the alveoli and the process is reversed as we breathe out air that now has a high carbon dioxide content.

Chemistry

This is the study of elements and compounds and the reactions they undergo. Which is a definition that surely cries out for a few definitions.

Element: a substance that cannot be resolved into a simpler substance by a chemical process. Groups of elements come together to form a **compound**. So, for example, a combination of the element hydrogen (H) and the element oxygen (O) can form the compound water (H_2O). (For an explanation of the $_2$, see p.98.)

Atom: the smallest particle in an element that can take part in a chemical reaction, made up of a **nucleus**, containing positively charged **protons** and neutral **neutrons**, and a number of **electrons**, negatively charged particles that orbit the nucleus. Each atom normally has the same number of protons and electrons, leaving it with a neutral charge. The movement of electrons is responsible for most commonly observed chemical, electrical or magnetic reactions. If an atom loses or gains an electron, it becomes either positively or negatively charged and is known as an **ion**.

Molecule: the smallest particle of a compound that can exist independently and retain its properties. So, in the example above, the smallest imaginable quantity of hydrogen and oxygen joined together in the right conditions and right proportions will still produce a molecule of water. Only when the hydrogen and oxygen are chemically separated again do they lose the properties that make them water and go back to being atoms of hydrogen and oxygen.

Mole: also known as Avogadro's number or Avogadro's constant, a mole contains the same number of particles as there are in 12g of carbon-12 atoms – that is, 6.022×10^{23} particles. Carbon is funny stuff – it has three naturally occurring isotopes (forms of the same substance with different numbers of neutrons),

PERIODIC TABLE OF THE ELEMENTS

1A		3B	4B	5B	6B	7B		8B		
1 **H** 1.00794 Hydrogen	2A									
3 **Li** 6.341 Lithium	4 **Be** 9.012182 Beryllium									
11 **Na** 22.989769 Sodium	12 **Mg** 24.3050 Magnesium									
19 **K** 39.0983 Potassium	20 **Ca** 40.078 Calcium	21 **Sc** 44.955912 Scandium	22 **Ti** 47.867 Titanium	23 **V** 50.9415 Vanadium	24 **Cr** 51.9961 Chromium	25 **Mn** 54.938045 Manganese	26 **Fe** 55.845 Iron	27 **Co** 58.933195 Cobalt	28 **Ni** 58.6934 Nickel	
37 **Rb** 85.4678 Rubidium	38 **Sr** 87.62 Strontium	39 **Y** 88.90585 Yttrium	40 **Zr** 91.224 Zirconium	41 **Nb** 92.90638 Niobium	42 **Mo** 95.96 Molybdenum	43 **Tc** [98] Technetium	44 **Ru** 101.07 Ruthenium	45 **Rh** 102.90550 Rhodium	46 **Pd** 106.42 Palladium	
55 **Cs** 132.9054519 Cesium	56 **Ba** 137.327 Barium	57-71 Lanthanides	72 **Hf** 178.49 Hafnium	73 **Ta** 180.94788 Tantalum	74 **W** 183.84 Tungsten	75 **Re** 186.207 Rhenium	76 **Os** 190.23 Osmium	77 **Ir** 192.217 Iridium	78 **Pt** 195.084 Platinum	
87 **Fr** [223] Francium	88 **Ra** [226] Radium	89-103 Actinides	104 **Rf** [267] Rutherfordium	105 **Db** [268] Dubnium	106 **Sg** [271] Seaborgium	107 **Bh** [272] Bohrium	108 **Hs** [270] Hassium	109 **Mt** [276] Meitnerium	110 **Ds** [281] Darmstadtium	

	57 **La** 138.90547 Lanthanum	58 **Ce** 140.116 Cerium	59 **Pr** 140.90765 Praseodymium	60 **Nd** 144.242 Neodymium	61 **Pm** [145] Promethium	62 **Sm** 150.36 Samarium	63 **Eu** 151.964 Europium
Lanthanides							
Actinides	89 **Ac** [227] Actinium	90 **Th** 232.03806 Thorium	91 **Pa** 231.03588 Protactinium	92 **U** 238.02891 Uranium	93 **Np** [237] Neptunium	94 **Pu** [244] Plutonium	95 **Am** [243] Americium

and one of these is carbon-12. I feel we might be getting into deep water here. See also *Avogadro's hypothesis*, p.108.

☞ **THE PERIODIC TABLE OF THE ELEMENTS**
The periodic table was first devised in 1889 by the Russian chemist Dimitri Mendeleyev, who was able to predict the existence of elements that had yet to be discovered because of the gaps that occurred. That's a bit clever, isn't it?

		3A	4A	5A	6A	7A	8A
							2 **He** 4.002602 Helium
		5 **B** 10.811 Boron	6 **C** 12.0107 Carbon	7 **N** 14.0067 Nitrogen	8 **O** 15.9994 Oxygen	9 **F** 18.9984032 Fluorine	10 **Ne** 20.1797 Neon
1B	2B	13 **Al** 26.9815386 Aluminum	14 **Si** 28.0855 Silicon	15 **P** 30.973762 Phosphorus	16 **S** 32.065 Sulfur	17 **Cl** 35.453 Chlorine	18 **Ar** 39.948 Argon
29 **Cu** 63.546 Copper	30 **Zn** 65.38 Zinc	31 **Ga** 69.723 Gallium	32 **Ge** 72.64 Germanium	33 **As** 74.92160 Arsenic	34 **Se** 78.96 Selenium	35 **Br** 79.904 Bromine	36 **Kr** 83.798 Krypton
47 **Ag** 107.8682 Silver	48 **Cd** 112.411 Cadmium	49 **In** 114.818 Indium	50 **Sn** 118.710 Tin	51 **Sb** 121.760 Antimony	52 **Te** 127.60 Tellurium	53 **I** 126.90447 Iodine	54 **Xe** 131.293 Xenon
79 **Au** 196.966569 Gold	80 **Hg** 200.59 Mercury	81 **Tl** 204.3833 Thallium	82 **Pb** 207.2 Lead	83 **Bi** 208.98040 Bismuth	84 **Po** [209] Polonium	85 **At** [210] Astatine	86 **Rn** [222] Radon
111 **Rg** [280] Roentgenium	112 **Uub** [285] Ununbium	113 **Uut** [284] Ununtrium	114 **Uuq** [289] Ununquadium	115 **Uup** [288] Ununpentium	116 **Uuh** [293] Ununhexium	117 **Uus** [294] Ununseptium	118 **Uuo** [294] Ununoctium

64 **Gd** 157.25 Gadolinium	65 **Tb** 158.92535 Terbium	66 **Dy** 162.500 Dysprosium	67 **Ho** 164.93032 Holmium	68 **Er** 167.259 Erbium	69 **Tm** 168.93421 Thulium	70 **Yb** 173.054 Ytterbium	71 **Lu** 174.9668 Lutetium
96 **Cm** [247] Curium	97 **Bk** [247] Berkelium	98 **Cf** [251] Californium	99 **Es** [252] Einsteinium	100 **Fm** [257] Fermium	101 **Md** [258] Mendelevium	102 **No** [259] Nobelium	103 **Lr** [262] Lawrencium

It arranges the elements in ascending order of **atomic number** (the number of protons that each possesses) in such a way that the vertical columns contain groups or families with similar chemical properties. The horizontal rows represent periods, with the most electropositive (an alkali metal) on the left and the so-called inert gases on the right, and the whole thing proves that 'the chemical properties of the elements are periodic functions of their atomic weights' – or, in other words, that similar properties in an element recur at regular intervals.

The elements are traditionally designated by a one- or two-letter abbreviation, as you can see in the table, and there are 117 of them, listed here with their atomic numbers:

1	Hydrogen	H	14	Silicon	Si
2	Helium	He	15	Phosphorus	P
3	Lithium	Li	16	Sulphur	S
4	Beryllium	Be	17	Chlorine	Cl
5	Boron	B	18	Argon	Ar
6	Carbon	C	19	Potassium	K
7	Nitrogen	N	20	Calcium	Ca
8	Oxygen	O	21	Scandium	Sc
9	Fluorine	F	22	Titanium	Ti
10	Neon	Ne	23	Vanadium	V
11	Sodium	Na	24	Chromium	Cr
12	Magnesium	Mg	25	Manganese	Mn
13	Aluminium	Al	26	Iron	Fe

27	Cobalt	Co	56	Barium	Ba
28	Nickel	Ni	57	Lanthanum	La
29	Copper	Cu	58	Cerium	Ce
30	Zinc	Zn	59	Praseodymium	Pr
31	Gallium	Ga	60	Neodymium	Nd
32	Germanium	Ge	61	Promethium	Pm
33	Arsenic	As	62	Samarium	Sm
34	Selenium	Se	63	Europium	Eu
35	Bromine	Br	64	Gadolinium	Gd
36	Krypton	Kr	65	Terbium	Tb
37	Rubidium	Rb	66	Dysprosium	Dy
38	Strontium	Sr	67	Holmium	Ho
39	Yttrium	Y	68	Erbium	Er
40	Zirconium	Zr	69	Thulium	Tm
41	Niobium	Nb	70	Ytterbium	Yb
42	Molybdenum	Mo	71	Lutetium	Lu
43	Technetium	Tc	72	Hafnium	Hf
44	Ruthenium	Ru	73	Tantalum	Ta
45	Rhodium	Rh	74	Tungsten	W
46	Palladium	Pd	75	Rhenium	Re
47	Silver	Ag	76	Osmium	Os
48	Cadmium	Cd	77	Iridium	Ir
49	Indium	In	78	Platinum	Pt
50	Tin	Sn	79	Gold	Au
51	Antimony	Sb	80	Mercury	Hg
52	Tellurium	Te	81	Thallium	Tl
53	Iodine	I	82	Lead	Pb
54	Xenon	Xe	83	Bismuth	Bi
55	Caesium	Cs	84	Polonium	Po

85	Astatine	At		102	Nobelium	No
86	Radon	Rn		103	Lawrencium	Lr
87	Francium	Fr		104	Rutherfordium	Rf
88	Radium	Ra		105	Dubnium	Db
89	Actinium	Ac		106	Seaborgium	Sg
90	Thorium	Th		107	Bohrium	Bh
91	Protactinium	Pa		108	Hassium	Hs
92	Uranium	U		109	Meitnerium	Mt
93	Neptunium	Np		110	Darmstadtium	Ds
94	Plutonium	Pu		111	Roentgenium	Rg
95	Americium	Am		112	Ununbium	Uun
96	Curium	Cm		113	Ununtrium	Uut
97	Berkelium	Bk		114	Ununquadium	Uuq
98	Californium	Cf		115	Ununpentium	Uup
99	Einsteinium	Es		116	Ununhexium	Uuh
100	Fermium	Fm		118	Ununoctium	Uuo
101	Mendelevium	Md				

From 93 upwards the elements don't occur naturally, but have been synthesized in particle accelerators. The last few are recent achievements and they have temporary names based on their atomic numbers. Element 117, which will be called Ununseptium, hasn't been synthesized yet, but they're working on it. What a strange job.

The lanthanides and actinides are usually separated from the rest of the table as shown, because – unlike the other rows – they have similar properties as you read across.

☞ ACIDS, BASES AND SALTS

An **acid** is defined as a substance (often sour and corrosive) that contains hydrogen atoms that, when the acid is dissolved in water, dissociate into ions and may be replaced by metals to form a salt.

A **base** is a compound that combines with an acid to form a salt plus water. Bases that are soluble in water are called **alkalis**. Many bases are oxides (so their formula ends in O, possibly with a little number after it) or hydroxides (OH).

A **salt** is a (usually crystalline) solid compound formed from the combination of an acid and a base by the replacement of hydrogen ions in the acid by positive ions in the base.

For example, combine sulphuric acid with the base cupric oxide in the right conditions and you get copper sulphate (that lovely bright blue stuff) and water:

$$H_2SO_4 + CuO \longrightarrow CuSO_4 + H_2O$$

In a school lab you test whether a substance is an acid or a base with litmus paper. Acid turns litmus red, bases turn it blue. Serious scientists use the **pH** – potential of hydrogen – which is measured by sensors and electrodes and things like that. Pure water has a pH of 7, with anything less being acidic and anything higher alkaline. Gardeners use this as a way of testing soil; you also sometimes see it on shampoo bottles.

Another term you might remember – and worth throwing in here – is **valency**, which means the number of atoms of hydrogen that an atom or group displaces when forming a compound. Hydrogen has a valency of one and oxygen a valency of two, which is why the formula for water is H_2O and not just HO – because you need two atoms of hydrogen to 'match' one of oxygen. Copper can have either of two valencies, which is why the one I mentioned a moment ago is called cupric oxide, not just copper oxide. There's also cuprous oxide, CuO_2.

☞ OXIDATION

Oxidation is a commonly quoted chemical reaction and the most common example of it is rust. In fact, anything that reacts when it comes into contact with oxygen is being subjected to oxidation: the green coating on an old copper coin is the result of oxidation; the browning of fruit is caused by oxygen burning away at the stuff that is released when you peel off the protective skin. Rust is, strictly speaking, the oxide that forms on iron or steel. Stainless steel doesn't rust because it is protected by a layer of chromium, which doesn't react to oxygen in the same way.

☞ DIFFUSION AND OSMOSIS

Molecules are constantly in motion and tend to move from regions where they are in higher concentration to regions where they are less concentrated – a process known as **diffusion**. Diffusion can occur in gases, in liquids or through solids.

Osmosis is a form of diffusion that is specific to the movement of water. Water moves through a selectively permeable membrane (that is, one that lets some types of molecules through, but not others) from a place where there is a higher concentration of water to one where it is lower.

In any form of diffusion, when the molecules are even throughout a space, they have reached **equilibrium**.

☞ BOILING AND FREEZING POINTS

If the temperature is low enough, every known substance except helium becomes a solid. The temperature at which this happens is called its **freezing point**. Above its freezing point, a substance is a liquid. At the other end of the scale, if the temperature is high enough, it becomes a gas, and this is called the **boiling point.**

Solid is the only state in which a substance retains its shape; a liquid assumes the shape of its container but does not necessarily fill it; a gas expands to fill the space available.

Think of water. In its solid state, it is ice and retains its shape – whether ice cube, icicle or iceberg – until the temperature rises sufficiently for it to melt and become liquid (water). If you take a tray of melted ice cubes and pour the water into a pan, it will take the shape of the container – that is, spread out to cover the bottom – but it may only come a certain distance up the side. If, however, you then turn on the heat under the pan, put a lid on it and boil the water, it will turn into gas (steam), fill the pan completely and probably seep out under the lid as well.

Non-scientists commonly measure temperature according to one of two scales: Celsius and Fahrenheit, both named after the people who invented them. Celsius used also to be called centigrade, from the Latin for *one hundred degrees*.

The freezing point of water is 0°C and its boiling point is 100°C. The equivalent in Fahrenheit is 32°F and 212°F. This means that the difference between freezing and boiling is 100°C and 180°F (212–32).

To convert Celsius to Fahrenheit you need to divide by 100 and multiply by 180, which can also be expressed as multiplying by 1.8, or $^9/_5$. Then, because the freezing point of water is 32°F, not 0°F, you need to add 32.

$$15°C \times 1.8 = 27; \ 27+32 = 59°F$$

To reverse the process, first deduct 32 from your Fahrenheit temperature, then divide by $^9/_5$ (or multiply by $^5/_9$, it's the same thing):

$$104°F-32 = 72; \ 72 \times {^5/_9} = 40°C$$

This works for any temperature above freezing.

There are two other scales used by scientists, the Réaumur and the Kelvin. According to Réaumur, water freezes as 0° and boils at 80° (because it just does, OK? – it's his scale, he makes the rules). Kelvin is interesting because he invented the concept of absolute zero, a temperature at which particles cease to have any energy – so, a scientific impossibility, although in the laboratory scientists have achieved temperatures within a millionth of a degree of it. Absolute zero is 0°K, or –273.15°C, which is pretty darned cold. I'd cease to have any energy at that temperature if I were a particle.

Physics

This is the one that deals with the properties and inter-actions of matter and energy, but its remit is constantly being redefined as we discover more stuff.

☞ OPTICS

Optics is all about light and has a few terms that may ring a bell.

Remember 'the angle of incidence equals the angle of reflection'? Of course you do. But do you remember what it means? Well, the **angle of incidence** is the angle at which light hits a surface; with **specular** (mirror-like) reflection, the light is reflected at the same angle. If the surface is rough, you get **diffuse** reflection, which means that the light bounces off in all directions.

Light may also pass through a medium – such as glass or water – and be **refracted** (change direction). This is because of the difference in the velocity with which light passes through the two different media (say air and water), which is measured by the **refractive index**.

☞ CONDUCTION, CONVECTION AND RADIATION

There are three ways in which heat is transferred. **Conduction** can occur in solids, liquids or gases and means (more or less) that a cool thing is warmed up by coming into contact with a hot thing.[9] The different levels of conductivity in metals are reflected in their uses in anything from the science lab to kitchenware: copper, for example, is highly conductive and therefore good for fast cooking (although it may react with certain foods, which is why copper-bottomed pans are often lined with tin); whereas cast iron heats slowly but then cooks evenly.

Convection occurs in liquids and gases and is the basis of the principle that hot air rises. A hot liquid or gas is generally less dense than a cool one; as the hot particles rise, cooler ones rush in underneath to take their place. As the hot particles rise, they cool and come down again, and so on.

Radiation involves the energy that all objects, hot or cold, emit. It is the only one of the three that works in a vacuum

---

9 Actually, it's to do with vibrating molecules and kinetic energy, but do you really want to go there?

and is how the sun's rays manage to warm the earth from all that distance away.

Heat is not the only commodity that is transferred in these ways: there is also electrical conduction, mass convection (of which evaporation is an example) and electromagnetic radiation. So, strictly speaking, you should put the words 'heat' or 'thermal' in front of 'conduction', 'convection' and 'radiation', if that is what you mean.

Physical laws

Physics is full of laws that tell us what matter and energy can or can't do, and doubtless without them the universe would fall apart. Some of them are below. But I guess a few definitions might help first:

Mass is the quantity of matter a body contains. Newton defined it more precisely by bringing in inertia, which is 'a property of matter by which it continues in its existing state of rest or uniform motion in a straight line, unless that state is changed by an external force'. They make it so complicated, don't they? All it means is that a thing will sit still until you push it.

Force is calculated by multiplying mass by acceleration, and is to do with producing motion in a stationary body or changing the direction of a moving one.

Velocity is speed (the dictionary says 'measure of the rate of movement' – but I call that 'speed') in a given direction.

Acceleration is the rate of increase in velocity.

Work is the exertion of force overcoming resistance (which might be electrical resistance, see below, or physical resistance, such as friction).

And, whatever anyone else tells you, in this context a **body** is a thing. The dictionary says, 'an object or substance that has three dimensions, a mass and is distinguishable from surrounding objects'. Come off it, say I, it's a thing.

Right, back to the laws.

☞ THE LAWS OF THERMODYNAMICS

Thermodynamics is the study of heat and its relationship with other forms of energy, and it is important in the study of heat engines such as petrol-driven motors and gas turbines. The other key term here is **entropy**, which is defined as 'a measure of the disorder of a system. Thus a solid has less entropy than a liquid since the constituent particles in a solid are in a more ordered state.'

Are you with me so far? OK. So, the three laws of thermodynamics state:

1 The energy of a closed system remains constant during any process, i.e. in a closed system, energy cannot be created or

destroyed, only transformed from one form into another.
(A closed system is just a posh way of saying 'other things
being equal' – as long as there are no outside influences
involved.)

2 Heat cannot flow spontaneously from a cold body to a hot
body (it can do this only with the help of an external agent,
such as the compressor in a fridge). Or, the entropy of a
closed system can never decrease.

3 As the thermodynamic temperature of a system approaches
absolute zero (see under *Boiling and freezing points*, p.99)
its entropy approaches zero.

Moving swiftly on.

☞ THE LAWS OF CONSERVATION OF ENERGY
AND MASS

Nothing to do with endangered species, the most common of
these states that energy in a closed system cannot be created or
destroyed (i.e. it's similar to the first law of thermodynamics),
and nor can mass. At a more advanced level, similar laws apply
to electric charge, linear momentum and angular momentum,
but I never got that far.

☞ NEWTON'S THREE LAWS OF MOTION

1 A body remains at rest or moves with constant velocity in a
straight line unless acted upon by a force.

2 The acceleration (*a*) of a body is proportional to the force (*f*) causing it: $f = ma$, where *m* is the mass of the body in question.

3 The action of a force always produces a reaction in the body, which is of equal magnitude but opposite in direction to the action.

Newton, of course, also came up with a **law of gravity**, which is that the force between two bodies is directly proportional to the product of their masses and inversely proportional to the square of the distance between them. The universal gravitational constant that makes this equation work is called *G* and its value is (wait for it) 6.673×10^{-11} newton metre squared per kilogram squared. (I know, I know.)

However, Einstein's general theory of relativity describes gravity more accurately. (More accurately than 6.673×10^{-11}?? Do we really need anything more accurate than that?)

☞ EINSTEIN'S THEORIES OF RELATIVITY

Before we consider Einstein's general theory of relativity, we have to look at his *special* theory of relativity. Before Einstein – that is, until the start of the twentieth century – it was believed that the speed of light relative to an observer could be calculated in the same way as the relative speed of any other two objects (such as two cars driving at different speeds). Einstein's theory is based on the assumption that the speed of light in a vacuum is a constant (2.998×10^8 metres – or 186,000 miles – per second), no matter whether or at what speed the observer is moving. Furthermore, he suggested that, as bodies increased in speed, they increased in mass and decreased in length – although this effect became noticeable only as objects neared the speed of light. All this led him to the conclusion that mass and energy were two different aspects of the same thing, which led to the famous equation

$$E = mc^2$$

where E is energy, m is mass and c is the velocity of light.

So, back to gravity. The special theory of relativity concerned motion in which there was no acceleration – that is, a constant speed. The general theory extended this to consider accelerated motion. According to this, gravity is a property of space and time that is 'curved' by the presence of a mass. Einstein posited that the motion of the stars and planets was controlled by this curvature of space in the vicinity of matter, and that light was also bent by the gravitational field of a massive body. Subsequent experiments have shown him to be right. Which is, I'm sure, a great relief to us all.

☞ OTHER LAWS
There are a handful of laws to do with gases:

Boyle's law states that, at constant temperature, the pressure of a gas is inversely proportional to its volume – the smaller a space it has to occupy, the more pressurized it is. This is only approximately true of real gases, and completely true only of 'ideal' or 'perfect' gases, which are a hypothetical concept. I wonder how many physicists have spent their careers investigating entirely hypothetical concepts.

Charles's law states that the volume of a gas at constant pressure is directly proportional to its temperature, or that gases expand by $^1/_{237}$ of their volume at 0°C for every 1°C increase in temperature. But, again, this is only approximately true.

Avogadro's hypothesis states that equal volumes of all gases at the same temperature and pressure contain the same number of molecules. This is sometimes called a law, but isn't really, because we don't (as yet) have a way of counting gas molecules – or measuring volumes – with complete accuracy.

And one to do with electric current, **Ohm's law**, which states that the current (I) flowing through an element in a circuit is directly proportional to the voltage drop or potential difference (V) across it: $V = IR$, where R means resistance – anything that gets in the way of the flow of current. What this means, more or less, is that the greater the resistance (measured in ohms), the greater the voltage (measured in volts) required to push the current (measured in amps) through it.

☞ **EQUATIONS OF MOTION**
These are basic equations that describe the motion of a body moving with constant acceleration.

A body moving with constant acceleration (a) starts with an initial velocity (u) and achieves a final velocity (v) in a time of t seconds, covering a total distance s. If you know any three of these components you can work out the other two.

Acceleration can be expressed as

$$a = \frac{v-u}{t}$$

Distance travelled (s) is simply time multiplied by average speed, that is to say:

$$s = t\,\frac{(u+v)}{2}$$

These two equations – one for calculating acceleration and the other for calculating distance – are essentially all we know about the matter, but we can get some other equations by combining them.

For example, we can eliminate v from both of them. The first equation can be recast as

$$v = u+at$$

(multiply everything by t, then add u to both sides)

and the second as

$$v = \frac{2s}{t} - u$$

(multiply everything by 2, divide by t and deduct u from both sides)

This may sound complicated, but the point is to produce an equation which defines v. Just in case you want to calculate v, you understand… But we also now have two equations beginning 'v=', so we can put them together and deduce that

$$u + at = \frac{2s}{t} - u$$

which, after a bit of re-arranging, is equivalent to

$$s = ut + \frac{1}{2}at^2$$

This looks a bit more impressive, but it's not really telling us anything new.

Similarly, we could eliminate u from each of our original equations, yielding

$$s = vt - \frac{1}{2}at^2$$

Or eliminate *t* from them both, to show that

$$v^2 = u^2 + 2as$$

So, to give an example: if a body travelling at 30 metres per second (*u*) accelerates at 2 metres per second per second (*a*) for 10 seconds (*t*), it reaches a velocity (*v*):

$$v = at + u = (2 \times 10) + 30 = 50 \text{ metres per second}$$

$$s = ut + \tfrac{1}{2}at^2 = (30 \times 10) + (\tfrac{1}{2} \times 2 \times 10^2)$$
$$= 300 + 100 = 400 \text{ metres}$$

Average speed is distance travelled (*s*) divided by *t*, which in this instance is $^{400}/_{10} = 40$ metres per second. Which sounds reasonable, as it starts at 30 and ends up at 50.

My friend Bob, who explained all this to me, says that this isn't rocket science, unless you have a rate of acceleration equal to the force of gravity, in which case you are into the realm of projectiles and ballistics, which are – um – rocket science.

HISTORY

School history was oddly arbitrary. I did my early schooling in New Zealand and, in the fifth form, we learnt a lot – or so it seemed at the time – about Gladstone and Irish Home Rule. Then I came to England and my new classmates were horrified to discover that I had never heard of Palmerston, who, I later found out, had been Prime Minister a mere three years before Gladstone. I suppose the syllabus had to start and end somewhere, but it did seem to lack continuity.

Which may be why I have written this chapter as a series of lists. After all, if, as one of Alan Bennett's *History Boys* puts it, history is one f***ing thing after another, what better way to present it? And, given that if you remember one date in history it is likely to be 1066, what better place to start?

Kings and Queens of England/Britain

In this list, sons succeeded their fathers unless otherwise stated.

☞ **THE HOUSE OF NORMANDY**
William I (1066–87): the Conqueror, victor at the Battle of Hastings (see p.138). Responsible for the Domesday Book and the feudal system.

William II (1087–1100): William Rufus, famous for being shot in the New Forest by a man called William Tyrrel. The conspiracy theorists will tell you that William's brother Henry was in the New Forest on the same day...

Henry I (1100–1135): brother of the above. A rather undersung king (Shakespeare didn't write a play about him, for one thing), who actually extended the English empire a lot – winning Normandy back from his brother Robert and subjugating to a greater or lesser extent the king of Scotland, the various princes of Wales and sundry French noblemen.

Stephen (1135–1154): nephew of the above. Henry I died leaving only a daughter, Matilda or Maud, but his sister's son seized the throne in her place. The battles between them continued throughout Stephen's reign, but Matilda won out in the end: she was married to Geoffrey Plantagenet, Count of Anjou, and their son became the next king.

☞ **THE HOUSE OF PLANTAGENET**

Henry II (1154–89): son of Matilda and great-grandson of William I. The one who came into conflict with Thomas à Becket ('Who will rid me of this turbulent priest?').

Richard I (1189–99): the Lionheart, spent most of his reign abroad fighting the Crusades; the good king in the Robin Hood stories.

John (1199–1216): brother of the above, the wicked Prince John in the Robin Hood stories. So hopeless that the barons forced him to sign Magna Carta (see p.146).

Henry III (1216–72): another king whose barons revolted against him; this time they were led by Simon de Montfort, who effectively ruled England until he was killed at the battle of Evesham in 1265.

Edward I (1272–1307): conquered most of Wales and built all the castles along the border. Tradition has it that he captured the hearts of the sentimental Welsh by promising them 'a prince who could speak no English' – and presenting them with his six-month-old son. In fact, the future Edward II was seventeen when he was given the title Prince of Wales, which rather spoils the story. Edward I continued his wars into Scotland, where he died fighting Robert the Bruce.

Edward II (1307–27): a serious mismanager, defeated by Robert the Bruce at the battle of Bannockburn in 1314, he also alienated his barons by promoting his favourites (notably Piers Gaveston) to undeserved places in government. Eventually deposed by his wife, Isabella, and her lover, Roger Mortimer, Earl of March, and murdered in Berkeley Castle. The play about him is not by Shakespeare but by Christopher Marlowe.

Edward III (1327–77): an altogether more successful king, who started as he meant to go on by exiling his mother and executing March. Nonetheless he used the fact that Isabella was the daughter of the king of France to claim that throne for himself, thus starting the Hundred Years' War (see p.138). He outlived his eldest son, Edward, the Black Prince and was therefore succeeded by...

Richard II (1377–99): grandson of the above, who alienated the aristocracy – especially his uncle John of Gaunt, Duke of Lancaster – and exiled several of his barons, including his cousin Henry Bolingbroke, John of Gaunt's son. Unsurprisingly, the barons were all in favour of an invasion by Henry; Richard was deposed and ended his days imprisoned in Pontefract Castle, succeeded by...

☞ **THE HOUSE OF LANCASTER**

Henry IV (1399–1413): the Bolingbroke of the previous entry. His reign was marked by battles at home, particularly against the Welsh prince Owen Glendower and Henry Percy ('Hotspur') of Northumberland, who sided with the Scots against the English king.

Henry V (1413–22): Shakespeare's Prince Hal, the one who has merry dealings with Falstaff but then grows up and wins the battle of Agincourt (see p.24 and p.139).

Henry VI (1422–61, briefly restored 1470–71): came to the throne as a baby and was married to a woman known as 'the She-wolf of France' – never stood a chance. See the *Wars of the Roses*, p139.

☞ THE HOUSE OF YORK

Edward IV (1461–83, briefly deposed 1470–71): great-great-grandson of Edward III (well, yes, some of the claims to the throne around this time were pretty tenuous). Brought to the throne with the help of Richard Neville, Earl of Warwick ('Warwick the Kingmaker'), who subsequently transferred his allegiance to Henry VI and forced Edward into exile; Edward returned six months later, killed Warwick at the battle of Barnet and probably murdered Henry shortly afterwards.

Edward V (1483): king for only three months at the age of thirteen; traditionally murdered in the Tower along with his brother, Richard Duke of York ('the Princes in the Tower'). I say 'traditionally' because some of us think this is vicious Tudor propaganda (see *Richard III*, p.25).

Richard III (1483–85): uncle of the above. Shakespeare's wicked hunchback and mass murderer, or dependable Regent who looked after the country during his nephew's minority? You pays your money... Defeated at the battle of Bosworth by...

☞ THE HOUSE OF TUDOR

Henry VII (1485–1509): one of the dodgier claimants to the English throne (see the *Wars of the Roses*, p.139), Henry was a Lancastrian who secured his position by marrying Elizabeth of York, daughter of Edward IV. His other great political move was to marry his elder son Arthur to Catherine of Aragon, daughter of the king of Spain, thus sealing an alliance with that country. Unfortunately, Arthur promptly died, leaving Catherine free to marry his younger brother...

Henry VIII (1509–47): he of the six wives. It's been told often enough, but briefly: Catherine of Aragon failed to produce a healthy son and heir, and Henry used the excuse that she was his brother's widow (and therefore the marriage had been unlawful in the first place) to divorce her. The Pope would have none of it, so Henry broke away from the Catholic Church and founded his own set-up. He married Anne Boleyn, who also failed to produce a living son, beheaded her on the grounds of adultery and married in quick succession: Jane Seymour (who did produce a son but died as a result); Anne of Cleves (divorced); Catherine Howard (beheaded); and Catherine Parr (survived). Prominent politicians and churchmen of the reign, bizarrely all called Thomas, included Cardinal Wolsey, Sir Thomas More ('a man for all seasons'), Archbishop Cranmer and Thomas Cromwell.

Edward VI (1547–53): the son of Jane Seymour. An ardent Protestant, his reign is best remembered for the production of the prayer books that were the forerunners of the Church of England's *Book of Common Prayer*. A major contributor to the prayer books, by the way, was Cranmer, the only one of the Thomases to survive Henry VIII – he was burned at the stake as a heretic during the reign of...

Mary I (1553–58): elder sister of the above, daughter of Catherine of Aragon. Edward had actually bequeathed his throne to a distant cousin, Lady Jane Grey, rather than to his Catholic sister, but Jane was overthrown after a mere nine days and beheaded. Mary was married to Philip II of Spain in another short-lived attempt to forge an alliance between the two countries. It was during her reign that Calais, the last English possession in France, was lost and she said that when she was dead they would find 'Calais' written on her heart (though I can't find a record of the post mortem confirming whether they did or not).

Elizabeth I (1558–1603): sister of the above, daughter of Anne Boleyn. Incarnated by Glenda Jackson or Cate Blanchett, depending on how old you are. Often known as the Virgin Queen. Hmm. A great patron of the arts and of explorers: Shakespeare, Christopher Marlowe, Edmund Spenser, Ben Jonson, Francis Drake and Walter Raleigh all flourished during this reign. The defeat of the Spanish Armada (and thus of her former brother-in-law Philip II) was one of her finest hours: the speech 'I know I have the body of a weak and feeble woman, but I have the heart and stomach of a king' was made before that battle.

Meanwhile, north of the border, the Scottish nobles had rebelled against Elizabeth's sort-of-cousin Mary Queen of Scots (she was the granddaughter of Henry VIII's sister, who had married the king of Scotland) and forced her to abdicate. She fled to England, where Elizabeth had her imprisoned and where, for the next twenty years, she was the focus of Catholic plots to depose Elizabeth, who eventually had her beheaded at Fotheringay Castle. But, when Elizabeth died childless, the throne went to Mary's son…

☞ THE HOUSE OF STUART

James I (1603–25): who was already James VI of Scotland. I once read a book about the kings of Scotland that described the Stuarts as 'a dynasty so appalling that the Scots were even prepared to lend them to the English' and James was the first of them. The problem with the Stuarts was that they believed in the Divine Right of Kings, which meant that they thought they could do what they liked, and they simply weren't bright enough to get away with it. However, James did oversee a translation of the Bible that is still called 'the Authorized Version'; many of Shakespeare's plays and Francis Bacon's essays were written during his reign, so he wasn't all bad and he was certainly better than his son…

Charles I (1625–49): really did think he could do what he liked and was beheaded as a result (see *English Civil Wars*, p.140). Had a stutter. Lots of famous portraits of him by Van Dyck.

☞ THE COMMONWEALTH (1649–60)

Should strictly speaking be divided into the Commonwealth (1649–53) and the Protectorate (1653–59), because during the latter period Oliver Cromwell and (after his death) his son, Richard, were Lord Protectors of England. Oliver had been the leader of the Parliamentary faction against Charles I, a highly successful general responsible for the New Model Army. His ruthless suppression of rebels in Ireland is legendary to this day. His strict Puritanism has led to this being regarded as a period of rather gloomy moral rectitude. Richard Cromwell failed to maintain his father's position and was forced to abdicate. Which left the throne free for...

☞ THE HOUSE OF STUART RESTORED

Charles II (1660–85): son of Charles I. Known as the Merry Monarch, he was the lover of Nell Gwyn and many many more, and reintroduced such pleasures as the theatre, which had been banned under the Commonwealth – the bawdy plays known as Restoration Comedies date from this time. The Great Plague and the Great Fire of London occurred during his reign; the latter leading to much rebuilding of churches, notably St Paul's Cathedral, by Sir Christopher Wren. Admitting on his deathbed that he was a Catholic, Charles had known how to juggle the best interests of rival religious factions, unlike...

James II (1685–88): brother of the above, an ardent Catholic. Suppressed the Monmouth Rebellion, when the Duke of Monmouth, an illegitimate son of Charles II living in the Netherlands, invaded England to stake a Protestant claim to the throne. James's anti-Protestant activities then became more and more pronounced, until the British landowners and clergy invited...

William III (1688–1702) and **Mary II** (1688–94) to invade the country and depose the king. Mary was the daughter of James II; her husband was a Dutch Protestant prince who also happened to be James's nephew (his mother had been James's sister). James fled to France and was received at the (Catholic) court of Louis XIV; his attempt to regain his throne led to defeat at the Battle of the Boyne in Ireland, still celebrated by annual parades on 12 July. Subsequent attempts by James's son James (the Old Pretender) and grandson Charles (the Young Pretender, 'Bonnie Prince Charlie') to regain the throne were finally quashed at the Battle of Culloden in 1745. Supporters of their cause were known as Jacobites, from Jacobus, the Latin for James.

But I'm getting ahead of myself. Back to William and Mary, who died childless, leaving the throne to…

Anne (1702–14): sister of Mary. Most famous for having innumerable (seventeen!) children, only one of whom survived infancy and he died at the age of twelve. After this she signed the Act of Settlement, which designated her – you guessed it, Protestant – German relatives as her successors (complicated family history – let's just say that James I's daughter had married a German prince and leave it at that). The Parliaments of England and Scotland were united for the first time under Anne.

☞ THE HOUSE OF HANOVER
George I (1714–27): never really mastered English – or indeed England; he lived in Hanover for as much of the time as he could.

George II (1727–60): still not really a very hands-on king but has the distinction of being the last British king to lead his troops into battle.

George III (1760–1820): the mad one, grandson of the above. Also responsible for losing what until then had been called the American colonies (see *American War of Independence*, p.140).

George IV (1820–30): Prince Regent for the last ten years of his mad father's reign, the one after whom Regency styles of architecture (such as the Royal Crescent in Bath) are named. Played by Hugh Laurie in *Blackadder*. His only daughter died young, so the throne passed to…

William IV (1830–37): brother of the above. Although he had ten children by an actress called Mrs Jordan, he left no legitimate offspring and the throne passed to…

☞ **THE HOUSE OF SAXE-COBURG-GOTHA**
Victoria (1837–1901): niece of the above. At the time of writing, still the longest-reigning monarch (although Elizabeth II is now the oldest). Married her cousin, Albert of Saxe-Coburg and Gotha, who became known as the Prince Consort. Albert was a rigid moralist – not something the previous generation of the royal family had been noted for – and his influence brought about the era of 'Victorian values'. His early death sent his widow into a long period of seclusion and mourning, the subject of the film *Mrs Brown*. Many of their nine children made important diplomatic marriages, with the result that

most of the present royal houses of Europe are in some way descended from Queen Victoria.[10]

Edward VII (1901–10): had been a scandalous Prince of Wales (his many mistresses included the American actress Lillie Langtry), but as king became an able diplomatist and pretty well redeemed himself.

☞ **THE HOUSE OF WINDSOR**

George V (1910–36): king during World War I, the General Strike and the Great Depression, and regarded as a valuable political adviser during these crises.

Edward VIII (1936): renowned as a playboy as a young man (you remember 'I danced with a man who'd danced with a girl who'd danced with the Prince of Wales'? Well, he was that Prince of Wales), he wanted to marry an American divorcee named Wallis Simpson, which was simply not allowed as long as he remained king. So he abdicated after less than a year, they married, became the Duke and Duchess of Windsor and remained married until his death in 1972.

George VI (1936–52): brother of the above, king during World War II, when he and his wife Elizabeth (for over fifty years known as the Queen Mother) were inspirational figureheads.

---

10 Did you know that both Queen Elizabeth II and her husband, Prince Philip, are great-great-grandchildren of Queen Victoria? Now you do.

Elizabeth II (1952–): the present queen. Matriarch of a terribly dysfunctional family – you've probably read about them.

Presidents of the United States

At the time of writing there have been forty-three presidents of the United States of America. Here are some of the most interesting of them. (D = Democrat, R = Republican, parties that came into being around 1828 and 1854 respectively.)

George Washington (1789–97): commander-in-chief of the forces that rebelled against British rule in the 1770s, and president of the Constitutional Convention of 1787 that produced the blueprint of today's Constitution. Unanimously elected first President of the United States two years later. Probably didn't chop down a cherry tree or tell his father that he couldn't tell a lie, but the legend persists.

John Adams (1797–1801): another major figure in the War of Independence, known as the 'colossus of the debate' over the Declaration of Independence. Became America's first vice-president, then president after Washington's resignation.

Thomas Jefferson (1801–09): credited with drafting the Declaration of Independence, and something of a polymath, with an interest in architecture, science and gardening, to name but a few. Lived for seventeen years after ceasing to be president and became a respected elder statesman.

James Madison (1809–17): 'the father of the Constitution', having played a major role in the Constitutional Convention of 1787.

James Monroe (1817–25): promulgator of the Monroe Doctrine 'that the American continents are henceforth not to be considered as subjects for future colonization by any European power'.

John Quincy Adams (1825–29): son of John Adams. Secretary of State under Monroe and may actually have written the Monroe Doctrine. Also an anti-slavery campaigner.

Abraham Lincoln (R, 1861–65): Really was born in a log cabin. Gained national stature from his stance against slavery. His election to the presidency caused the Southern States to secede from the Union, thus beginning the Civil War (see p.140). His Gettysburg Address – 'Fourscore and seven years ago our fathers brought forth upon this continent a new nation, conceived in liberty...' – further expressed his anti-slavery views, as did his campaign for re-election in 1864. He was shot by John Wilkes Booth five days after the surrender of the Confederate general Robert E. Lee, which effectively ended the Civil War. (The surrender, I mean, not the assassination.)

Ulysses S. Grant (R, 1869–77): leader of the Union army during the Civil War; presided over the reconstruction of the South.

James Garfield (R, 1881): assassinated by a disgruntled office-seeker after only a few months in office.

William McKinley (R, 1897–1901): president during the war with Spain that saw the US acquire Cuba and the Philippines. Assassinated by an anarchist in Buffalo (I didn't know they had anarchists in Buffalo, but you're always learning).

Theodore Roosevelt (R, 1901–09): one of two US presidents to be awarded a Nobel Peace Prize (for his role in ending the Russo-Japanese War) – the other was Woodrow Wilson. Expansionist policies included promoting the growth of the US navy and the building of the Panama Canal. A great advocate of the US entering the First World War.

Woodrow Wilson (D, 1913–21): avoided joining the war for several years but in the end was forced to – 'to make the world safe for democracy'. His Fourteen Point plan to prevent future wars formed the basis of the League of Nations (the forerunner of the United Nations).

Warren Harding (R, 1921–23): campaigned on the issue of opposing US membership of the League of Nations; died in office, in mysterious circumstances.

Calvin Coolidge (1923–29): notoriously taciturn president, whose economic policies were blamed for the 1929 Wall Street Crash. The story goes that a woman sitting next to him at a dinner party bet him that she would get at least three words out of him in the course of the evening. 'You lose' was the president's reply – and she did: he didn't say another word for the rest of the night.

Franklin D. Roosevelt (D, 1933–45): the longest-serving president in US history. Stricken with polio and confined to a wheelchair throughout his presidency. Came to power at the height of the Great Depression and instituted the 'New Deal' for economic recovery. President during most of World War II, he died in office three weeks before Germany surrendered. His wife, Eleanor, was a noted diplomat and political adviser.

Harry S. Truman (D, 1945–53): Roosevelt's vice-president, succeeded him in the last months of World War II and was responsible for the decision to drop atomic bombs on Nagasaki and Hiroshima. Also popularized the expression 'The buck stops here.'

Dwight D. Eisenhower (R, 1953–61): Supreme Commander of the Allied forces during the 1944 Normandy landings; his presidency coincided with the height of the Cold War (see p.146) and the birth of the civil rights movement.

John F. Kennedy (D, 1961–63): the first Catholic, and still the youngest person, to be elected president. He and his glamorous wife, Jackie, changed the image of the presidency. President during the Cuban Missile Crisis, which may be the nearest the world has ever come to nuclear war. Assassinated in Dallas by Lee Harvey Oswald, who was himself shot and killed by

Jack Ruby two days later. The conspiracy theorists are still working on it.

Lyndon B. Johnson (D, 1963–69): Kennedy's vice-president. The Civil Rights Act and the Voting Rights Act, which extended the voting rights of African-Americans, were passed during his presidency, but Johnson is now mostly remembered for his escalation of the Vietnam War and the subsequent protests.

Richard Nixon (R, 1969–74): the only US president to resign under the threat of impeachment, following the scandal known as Watergate: the Democratic Party's headquarters at the Watergate Hotel had been burgled during the 1972 elections and it became apparent that Nixon knew all about it and the subsequent cover-up. *Washington Post* journalists Bob Woodward and Carl Bernstein led the exposure – the story is told in their book *All the President's Men* and the film based on it.

Gerald Ford (R, 1974–77): the only president not to have been elected, even as vice-president: Nixon appointed him after the elected VP, Spiro Agnew, resigned over a tax scandal. Remembered largely as the man said to be so dumb he couldn't walk and chew gum at the same time.

Jimmy Carter (D, 1977–81): the peanut farmer from Georgia who brought social reform at home and was instrumental in arranging a peace treaty between Israel and Egypt, but will be remembered for the chaos surrounding the taking of US hostages in the American Embassy in Iran.

Ronald Reagan (R, 1981–89): former Hollywood film star and long-term governor of California before becoming president. Introduced the anti-Russian Strategic Defence Initiative (known as Star Wars), but later reached an arms-reduction agreement with the USSR. Was wounded in an unsuccessful assassination attempt that provoked the remark, 'Honey, I forgot to duck.'

George Bush (R, 1989–93): took the world into the first Gulf War and invented the convoluted speech patterns known as 'Bushisms', which were perfected by his son, George W.

Bill Clinton (D, 1993–2001): young, charismatic and spent a lot of time in the headlines because of his alleged affair with a White House intern ('I did not have sexual relations with that woman'). Married to Hillary, who didn't get to be president this time round.

George W. Bush (R, 2001–09): still president at the time of writing. Better not say any more.

British Prime Ministers

So, moving down from heads of state to the next tier...

Tradition always starts this list with Robert Walpole, chief minister for twenty years under Georges I and II, although the term 'Prime Minister' was not in common use until Disraeli's time and not official until Campbell-Bannerman. Whatever you want to call him, Walpole was an exceptionally able man who happened to be around when there were two kings who didn't speak much English and didn't really care what was going on in their kingdom. He was succeeded by a number of people that no one remembers much about, the two early exceptions being:

William Pitt the Elder, 1st Earl of Chatham (1766–8, Whig[11]): known as 'the Great Commoner' (until he was made an earl, that is) and a renowned orator. Famously incorruptible.

Lord North (1770–82, Tory): remembered because he was in power at the time of the American Declaration of Independence and subsequent war.

It's right at the end of the eighteenth century that the Prime Ministers really become important, so let's just skip through most of them:

William Pitt the Younger (1783–1801, 1804–6, Tory): son of William Pitt the Elder. At twenty-four, the youngest Prime Minister ever and one of the most influential – introduced sweeping economic reforms, brought about parliamentary union with Ireland, formed an alliance with other European powers to fight Napoleon, culminating in victory at the Battle

---

11 Whigs and Tories were the forerunners of Liberals and Conservatives respectively. The first Labour MP, Keir Hardie, took his seat in 1892.

of Trafalgar. Also supported Catholic emancipation and resigned in 1801 in protest against George III's opposition. The first Prime Minister to live at 10 Downing Street. Immensely energetic and notoriously hard-drinking; burned himself out and died at forty-six.

Spencer Perceval (1809–12, Tory): the only British Prime Minister to be assassinated – shot by a bankrupt Liverpool broker while entering the lobby of the House of Commons.

George Canning (1827, Tory): best remembered for fighting a duel, when he was Minister for Foreign Affairs, with the Secretary for War, Lord Castlereagh, because of a disastrous incident in the Napoleonic Wars called the Walcheren Expedition. Prime Minister for only a few months, he died in office.

Duke of Wellington (1828–30, Tory): yes, *the* Duke of Wellington; a hard-line Tory, firmly opposed to the growing movement for parliamentary reform, although he went against the traditional party line by espousing the cause of Catholic emancipation.

Earl Grey (1830–34, Whig): the Reform Act of 1832, which gave the vote to a lot of men who hadn't had it before and disenfranchised some of the underpopulated 'rotten' boroughs, was Grey's doing. And the tea is named after him, yes.

Viscount Melbourne (1834, 1835–41, Whig): Prime Minister at the time of the accession of the young Queen Victoria and a mentor to her. Married to Lady Caroline Lamb, who made herself notorious through her affair with Byron.

Robert Peel (1834–5, 1841–6, Tory): reorganized the London police force, which is why they are still known as 'bobbies' and used to be known as 'peelers'. Also controversially repealed the Corn Laws, which had protected the interests of farmers by keeping the price of corn artificially high, but upset the poor by keeping the price of bread high, too. This action caused a split in the Tory party that led to the emergence of the Conservatives (under Disraeli). Peel's supporters, known as Peelites, joined forces with the Whigs and the Radicals, an odd alliance from which emerged the Liberal Party.

Earl of Derby (1852, 1858–9, 1866–8, Conservative): pushed through the Second Reform Act, which reduced the amount of property an enfranchised man had to own, or rent he had to pay, and thus gave the vote for the first time to quite a few of the working class. Still men only, of course.

Viscount Palmerston (1855–8, 1859–65, Liberal): a great orator and a notably xenophobic Foreign Secretary before he became Prime Minister. Forcefully anti-Russian during the Crimean War (see p.142), he didn't like the French, the Chinese or the Irish much, either.

Benjamin Disraeli (1868, 1874–80, Conservative): started his career as a novelist (*Sybil* and *Coningsby*), but was committed to social and politic climbing and grew to be Gladstone's great rival. A favourite of Queen Victoria, he contrived to make her 'Empress of India'.

William Ewart Gladstone (1868–74, 1880–85, 1886, 1892–94, Liberal): earnest and hardworking where Disraeli was flamboyant and diplomatic, he alienated Queen Victoria by speaking to her 'as if she were a public meeting'. An unsuccessful advocate of Irish Home Rule, his great achievement was the introduction of 'free, compulsory and secular' education for all. Remained in Parliament until he was well into his eighties and became known as the 'Grand Old Man', or GOM.

Marquis of Salisbury (1885–6, 1886–92, 1895–1902, Conservative): a member of the Cecil family, descended from Elizabeth I's adviser Lord Burghley. Extended British interests in Africa, including the establishment of Rhodesia (now Zimbabwe), whose capital was originally called Salisbury.

Earl of Rosebery (1894–5, Liberal): inherited a divided cabinet and a hostile House of Lords from Gladstone; lasted only fifteen months but was really more interested in his racehorses, anyway.

Arthur Balfour (1902–5, Conservative): nephew of Lord Salisbury, remembered principally for the Balfour Declaration of 1917 (when he was Foreign Secretary), which paved the way for the creation of the state of Israel thirty years later.

Henry Campbell-Bannerman (1905–8, Liberal): the first person officially to be called Prime Minister and the only PM actually to die in 10 Downing Street.

Herbert Asquith (1908–16, Liberal): introduced the act that limited the power of the House of Lords; 'We had better wait and see' became his catchphrase during the ensuing constitutional crisis. Formed a coalition government after the outbreak of World War I, but was soon ousted by supporters of...

David Lloyd George (1916–22, Liberal): 'the Welsh wizard', a great orator and notorious womanizer, saw Britain through the second half of World War I; some put his role on a par with that of Churchill in the Second. Afterwards, his negotiations with Sinn Fein led to the creation of the Irish Free State.

Andrew Bonar Law (1922–3, Conservative): the 'forgotten Prime Minister', in office for only seven months; nevertheless deemed important enough to be buried in Westminster Abbey.

Stanley Baldwin (1923, 1924–9, 1935–7, Conservative): a notoriously lazy man, he still had a busy time, being Prime Minister during the general strike of 1926, the beginnings of the great depression and the abdication crisis of 1936.

James Ramsay MacDonald (1924, 1929–35, Labour): the first ever Labour Prime Minister, became leader of the National (coalition) Government formed in 1931 after financial and political crises led to the collapse of the minority Labour administration.

Neville Chamberlain (1937–40, Conservative): remembered for his appeasement of Adolf Hitler; came back from Munich in 1938 waving a piece of paper and saying, 'There will be peace in our time.' Hmm.

Winston Churchill (1940–5, 1951–5, Conservative – though he spent twenty years with the Liberals from 1904–24): offered blood, toil, tears and sweat, fought on the beaches, fought on the landing grounds and never surrendered. He had been a war correspondent during the Boer War, First Lord of the Admiralty and later Minister of Munitions during World War I and was a prolific author (and winner of the Nobel Prize for Literature) and superb orator. His promotion to leader of the wartime Coalition government in 1940 had its detractors, but he became the single most important figurehead of the British resistance to Nazism. His cigars and 'V for Victory' live on in the memories of people far too young to remember them first hand.

Clement Attlee (1945–51, Labour): described by Churchill as 'a modest little man who has a great deal to be modest about', he nevertheless presided over the birth of the National Health Service and other aspects of the welfare state.

Anthony Eden (1955–7, Conservative): Prime Minister during the Suez Crisis: criticized by the United Nations and the British public for sending troops into the Canal Zone; by the time he ordered a withdrawal the damage to his reputation was done and politically he never recovered.

Harold Macmillan (1957–63, Conservative): two great quotes: 'Most of our people have never had it so good' (although this wasn't original – the US Democratic Party had used it as a campaign slogan some years before) and 'The wind of change is blowing through this continent', a speech in support of the many African states seeking independence at the time. He resigned on the grounds of ill health after the Profumo affair, of which it was said that 'the Prime Minister must not be brought down by the actions of two tarts.' Hmm.

Alec Douglas–Home (1963–4 Conservative): a surprise choice to succeed Macmillan, he renounced his hereditary peerage to take his place in the House of Commons. Resigned leadership of the Conservative Party after the election defeat that soon followed; later became a life peer with the wonderful title of Baron Home of the Hirsel.

Harold Wilson (1964–70, 1974–6, Labour): smoked a pipe, wore a raincoat, promised us that the pound in our pocket had not been devalued – when of course it had, or why would he have been talking about it? Also probably the first person to have said, 'A week is a long time in politics.'

Edward Heath (1970–4, Conservative): took Britain into the EC, despite speaking the worst French of anyone in public life, but at home had lots of conflict with the trade unions and at one stage put the country on to a three-day week to save power.

James Callaghan (1976–9, Labour): 'Sunny Jim'. Becoming Labour leader when Wilson suddenly resigned, he inherited a tiny majority and was soon dependent on a dodgy alliance with the Liberals. Presided over the 1978 'winter of discontent' brought on by widespread industrial action.

Margaret Thatcher (1979–90, Conservative): yes, yes, I know, first woman party leader, first woman Prime Minister, won the Falklands War, crushed the miners' strike, the lady who wasn't for turning, but will always be remembered by my generation as the 'milk snatcher' who discontinued the supply of free milk to primary-school children.

John Major (1990–97, Conservative): a surprise choice to succeed the Iron Lady; appeared as a grey puppet in *Spitting Image* and, after his retirement, became president of Surrey County Cricket Club and author of a book on the history of cricket. Always seems very happy when he is interviewed during the lunch interval of the Oval test.

Tony Blair (1997–2007, Labour) and **Gordon Brown** (2007–, Labour): too recent to have been taught in many schools. And still alive, so we have to be careful. Blair briefly presided over 'Cool Britannia' before the Iraq debacle, for which he will probably be best (if that's the word I want) remembered.

So what were all those wars about, then?

Power, territory and religion mostly.

☞ **1066:** BATTLE OF HASTINGS

The year 1066 was rather a busy one. King Edward the Confessor died on 5 January, leaving four claimants to the throne. The legitimate heir, Edward's son Edgar, was a child and no one took much notice of him. Military expediency preferred the successful Saxon general Harold Godwin, but there was also the Norwegian king, Harald Hardrada, who invaded northern England and, on 25 September, was defeated by the other Harold at Stamford Bridge, near York. Three days later, an army led by William of Normandy (to whom Harold Godwin may or may not have promised allegiance in a visit to Normandy the previous year) landed at Pevensey in Sussex, some 400 kilometres away. Harold marched to meet him, the battle now known as Hastings took place on 14 October, Harold was killed (tradition has it by an arrow in his eye) and, on Christmas Day, William 'the Conqueror' was crowned King William I.

☞ **1337–1453:** HUNDRED YEARS WAR

Between England and France. Primarily a dispute over territory because parts of France, notably the prosperous wine-growing areas of Gascony and Aquitaine, had come into English possession through a succession of strategic marriages. The most famous battles were all English victories, funnily enough (I wonder who was writing the books): Crécy (1346), at which Edward III's son, the Black Prince, 'won his spurs'; Poitiers (1356), when the French king, John II, was captured and held for ransom; and Harfleur and Agincourt (both 1415), when English archers won the day. After Henry V's early death in 1422, a French resurgence inspired by Joan of Arc gradually pushed the English back until in 1453 the French won a decisive victory at Castillon and reclaimed all of the southwest part of the country. Only Calais remained in English possession (see *Mary I*, p.117).

☞ 1455–1485: WARS OF THE ROSES

Between the English royal houses of York and Lancaster. To put it in a nutshell, Edward III had far too many descendants who thought they ought to be in charge. Key battles were Wakefield (1460), in which Richard Duke of York, leader of the opposition to the Lancastrian Henry VI, was killed; Tewkesbury (1471), a Yorkist victory, shortly after which Henry VI died – probably murdered – in the Tower of London. Rivalry between the new (Yorkist) king Edward IV's in-laws, the numerous and opportunistic Woodvilles, and other members of the aristocracy ensured that conflict continued and culminated in the Battle of Bosworth (1485), when Henry Tudor, a Lancastrian descended from an illegitimate son of Edward III's son, John of Gaunt, defeated and killed the Yorkist Richard III and became Henry VII.

☞ **1588:** DEFEAT OF THE SPANISH ARMADA

Claiming divine authority for his actions, the Catholic Philip II of Spain sent a fleet ('armada' in Spanish) of 130 ships to invade Protestant England. In a number of encounters in the Channel it was soundly defeated by Elizabethan admirals including Sir Francis Drake and Sir John Hawkins.

☞ **1642–51:** ENGLISH CIVIL WARS

The culmination of a conflict between king and Parliament (whose faction became known as Roundheads) that had been going on for years (see the *House of Stuart*, p.119) and was precipitated when Charles I rejected Parliament's demands for reform, known as the Nineteen Propositions. The first (indecisive) battle was at Edgehill in 1642; Charles was defeated at Marston Moor in 1644, Naseby in 1645 and Newark in 1646, after which he surrendered to the Scots. He later escaped to the Isle of Wight, sparked off another couple of years of war and was finally beheaded in 1649.

☞ **1775–83:** AMERICAN WAR OF INDEPENDENCE OR AMERICAN REVOLUTION

Clue in the title, really. The thirteen British colonies in North America revolted against British rule, specifically against what they saw as unfair taxation. The Boston Tea Party (1773) was an act of defiance in the run-up to open warfare. Early battles at Lexington and Concord were followed by the Declaration of Independence (1776) and battles across what are now the north-eastern United States and eastern Canada. George Washington was the American commander-in-chief, Generals Burgoyne and Cornwallis key figures on the British side. France, Spain and Holland all sided with the Americans – the Dutch even gained control of the Channel and threatened to invade Britain. Britain finally acknowledged American independence by the Treaty of Paris (1783).

☞ 1789: FRENCH REVOLUTION

Like the English with the Stuarts 150 years earlier, the French finally had enough of the Bourbon kings and overthrew them, storming the state prison, the Bastille, on 14 July, mobbing the palace of Versailles and eventually beheading King Louis XVI and his queen, Marie Antoinette. The revolutionaries proclaimed a republic, but the moderate Girondins were ousted by the more extreme Jacobins and power passed to the hands of the Committee of Public Safety (one of those names that you can just tell is going to lead to trouble). Danton, initially one of the most important members of the Committee, was superseded by Robespierre, and the ensuing Reign of Terror saw the execution of thousands of alleged anti-revolutionaries. Perhaps inevitably, Danton and Robespierre both also ended up on the guillotine.

☞ 1792–1815: NAPOLEONIC WARS

Napoleon Bonaparte rose to prominence in the aftermath of the French Revolution, was in charge of the French army fighting the Austrians in Italy by 1796, and then took it into his head to break down the British Empire by conquering Egypt. Defeated by Nelson at the battle of the Nile (1799), he returned to France, overthrew the Directoire (the post-revolutionary government), became consul and then Emperor in 1804, when he was all of thirty-five. The following year he was again defeated by Nelson (at Trafalgar, where Nelson was killed), but did better on land, winning victories at Austerlitz, Jena and Friedland and more or less conquering continental Europe. The Duke of Wellington defeated him in the Iberian Peninsula – a sub-section of the Napoleonic Wars known as the Peninsular War (1808–14), in the course of which Napoleon also found time to march on Moscow, losing about 400,000 of his 500,000-strong army in the harsh Russian winter. He was defeated again at Leipzig in 1814, forced to abdicate and exiled to Elba, an island off the coast of Italy. He escaped, resumed power for the 'Hundred Days', was finally defeated in 1815 at the battle of Waterloo and exiled again, this time to the remote South Atlantic island of St Helena, where he died in 1821.

☞ 1853–56: CRIMEAN WAR

Britain, France and the Ottoman (Turkish) Empire vs Russia, sparked by Russia's desire to expand its territory into the Balkans (south-eastern Europe, at that time part of the Ottoman Empire). Key events are the siege of Sevastopol, the battle of Balaclava and the Charge of the Light Brigade, a catastrophic error of judgement on the part of the British commanders,

Lords Raglan and Cardigan. 'Into the valley of Death rode the six hundred,' Tennyson wrote, and indeed about 250 of them were killed. Despite this managerial incompetence, the massive loss of life on both sides throughout the war was attributed largely to the appalling quality of the field hospitals: enter Florence Nightingale.

☞ 1861–65: AMERICAN CIVIL WAR

Between the Federal government and the eleven breakaway Confederate states, who objected to the anti-slavery policies of Abraham Lincoln. The Confederate secession was led by Jefferson Davis and the war began with a Confederate attack on Port Sumner, Virginia. Later key encounters were the Confederate victory at Bull Run, the Confederate general Stonewall Jackson's campaign in Shenandoah, the Federal victories in the Seven Days' Battle and at Gettysburg and their capture of Atlanta and Savannah. Robert E. Lee was the other great Confederate general; the Federal leaders included William Sherman and the future president Ulysses S. Grant.

☞ 1880–81 AND 1899–1902: BOER WARS

Revolutionary wars fought by the Afrikaners (Boers, descended from Dutch settlers) of South Africa against British rule. The first, in which the Boers were led by Kruger, gained a degree of independence for Transvaal, which became known as the South African Republic. The second involved lengthy Boer sieges of Ladysmith and Mafeking. Kitchener was one of the leaders of the British forces; Baden-Powell, who went on to found the Boy Scouts, distinguished himself in the siege of Mafeking. British public and political opinion was polarized by the second Boer War and it led to a lot of rising and falling of governments.

☞ 1914–18: WORLD WAR I

The principal players were an alliance of Britain, France, Russia and others (the Allied Powers, united by the Entente Cordiale and later the Triple Entente), against Germany, Austro-Hungary and Turkey (the Central Powers); the USA joined in 1917. The complicated causes included the Allies' fear of German expansion in Europe and various colonies, particularly in Africa; and a conflict of interest between Russia and Austro-Hungary in the Balkans. Although war was looming for years, it was sparked by the assassination of the Archduke Franz Ferdinand, heir to the Austro-Hungarian throne, by a Serb nationalist, Gabriel Princip. Austro-Hungary declared war on Serbia, Russia backed the Serbs and you can guess the rest. Much of the war took place on what is known as the Western Front in the trenches of north-eastern France and Belgium, and is most notable for the horrific loss of life: over a million men in the Battle of the Somme alone, with Ypres and Passchendaele not much better. On the Eastern Front, the Gallipoli campaign in Turkey killed a lot of Australians and New Zealanders.

☞ 1917: RUSSIAN REVOLUTION

Actually two revolutions, one in February, one in October of the same year. The first, sparked by shortage of food, led to the abdication of the Romanov Tsar Nicholas II; the second involved the Bolsheviks (led by Lenin and Trotsky) seizing power, executing most of the royal family and establishing the first communist state. A civil war between the 'Red' Bolsheviks and the anti-communist 'White' Russians lasted until 1921. After Lenin died in 1924, Trotsky lost a power struggle with Stalin, went into exile in Mexico and was murdered there (with an ice pick in his head).

☞ 1939–45: WORLD WAR II

Hitler rose to power in Germany in the early 1930s and proceeded to take over various parts of Europe. Britain and France had promised to protect Polish neutrality, so were forced to declare war when Germany invaded Poland. Hitler's invasion of France led to the evacuation of hundreds of thousands of Allied forces, many of them in small boats, from Dunkirk, in 1940; Britain now faced the threat of invasion and months of bombing ('the Blitz'). The war in the air that followed (1940–1) is what is known as the Battle of Britain. In December 1941, the Japanese bombed the Hawaiian naval base at Pearl Harbour, bringing the USA into the war and opening up a whole new theatre of conflict in the Pacific. The Normandy (D-Day) landings in June 1944 began the turning of the tide against Germany, which surrendered in May 1945. In August, the dropping of atomic bombs first on Hiroshima, then three days later on Nagasaki, forced the Japanese to surrender.

☞ THE COLD WAR

Difficult to date because it wasn't really a war, but a period of intense mutual distrust between former World War II allies the USA, UK and France on the one hand and the USSR on the other, at its height during the 1950s. Winston Churchill coined the term 'iron curtain' for the ideological and political barrier that separated east from west. This began to relax in the 1970s and 1980s, especially with the introduction by Mikhail Gorbachev of the policies of *glasnost* (openness) and *perestroika* (reconstruction – specifically of the economy) which led to the break up of the USSR.

A few more important dates

This small section just didn't fit anywhere else, but most of us will remember at least something about these events:

☞ 1215: MAGNA CARTA, OR THE GREAT CHARTER

Signed by King John at Runnymede, this was the first successful attempt to control the power of the English monarchy.

☞ 1453: FALL OF CONSTANTINOPLE

You might not think it was any big deal (after all, cities were falling all over the place all the time), but this was when the (Muslim) Turks took over the (Christian) capital of the Eastern Roman Empire and all those scholarly monks fled into Western Europe, taking their books with them. In other words, it marked the start of the Renaissance – which, in its narrowest sense, means a rebirth in interest in classic literature, art and architecture.

☞ 1605: GUNPOWDER PLOT

A completely incompetent attempt by a group of Catholics to blow up the Protestant King James I and the Houses of Parliament. Somebody grassed and Guy Fawkes – who is the reason we burn 'guys' on 5 November – was caught in the cellars under the Palace of Westminster with a load of gunpowder. No prizes for guessing what happened to him.

☞ 1620: PILGRIM FATHERS

A group of Puritans, persecuted in England because of their religion, set sail in the *Mayflower* and in due course established the first colony in Plymouth, Massachusetts.

☞ EARLY EIGHTEENTH CENTURY ONWARDS: AGRICULTURAL REVOLUTION

Larger enclosed fields, inventions such as Jethro Tull's planting drill, and the concept of crop rotation pioneered by Viscount 'Turnip' Townshend improved agricultural methods and increased food yield, which made it possible to feed the increasing numbers of people working other than on the land following the Industrial Revolution.

☞ **1750 ONWARDS: INDUSTRIAL REVOLUTION**
The invention of Arkwright's water-powered spinning frame, Hargreaves' spinning jenny and Crompton's mule revolutionized the production of yarn and therefore cloth, leading to the development of factories and mass production.

Explorers

And just for fun, because we have been talking about fighting over lots of parts of the world, here is a quick rundown of people who discovered some of them.

Eric the Red and **Leif Eriksson** (late 10th–11th century, Norwegian): father and son. Eric, brought up in Iceland, was the first European to settle in Greenland; Leif, blown (a long way) off course on his way from Iceland to Greenland, became the first European to reach America. He landed at a place he called Vinland, which may have been modern-day Newfoundland or Nova Scotia.

Bartolomeu Dias (*c.*1450–*c.*1500, Portuguese): trade routes to India were the big thing after the Turks blocked off the land route. Dias made a game stab at doing it by sea, being the first to round the Cape of Good Hope at the bottom of Africa.

But he named it the Cape of Storms, which may suggest why his crew made him turn back before they got further than Mozambique.

Christopher Columbus (1451–1506, Italian): born in Genoa, but had his voyages sponsored by Ferdinand and Isabella of Spain. The idea was to reach the East (that is, Asia) by sailing west, thus proving beyond all doubt that the Earth was round. Of course, America got in the way. Columbus never actually reached mainland North America, but did discover the Bahamas, Hispaniola, Guadeloupe, Jamaica and Puerto Rico, among others. His ships were the *Santa Maria*, the *Niña* and the *Pinta*.

Amerigo Vespucci (1454–1512, Italian): discovered the mouth of the Amazon and the River Plate, which somehow made him important enough to have a continent or two named after him.

Vasco da Gama (*c.*1469–1525, Portuguese): persisted where Dias had failed and made it to Calicut in India.

Francisco Pizarro (*c.*1478–1541, Spanish): the conqueror (or *conquistador*) of Peru and destroyer of the Incan Empire.

Ferdinand Magellan (*c.*1480–1521, Portuguese): leader of the first expedition to sail round the world, although he himself was murdered in the East Indies. Like Columbus he was trying to reach the East by sailing west, and this took him through the Straits of Magellan at the southern tip of South America.

Hernán Cortés (1485–1547, Spanish): did for the Aztecs in Mexico (whose emperor was Montezuma) much the same as Pizarro had done in Peru.

Francis Drake (1540–96, English): best known of the Elizabethan seafarers who were in constant battle with the Spaniards over control of the Caribbean (the 'Spanish Main') and its riches – they would have been described as pirates if they hadn't been on our side. Drake – in a ship called the *Pelican*, later renamed the *Golden Hind* – was the first Englishman to sail round the world; he was also pivotal in the English defeat of the Spanish Armada (see p.140).

James Cook (1728–79, British): one of the great navigators of all time, made three expeditions to the Pacific in an attempt to discover the supposed great southern continent. He became the first European to land in New Zealand and also charted parts of Australia and Antarctica. His famous ships were the *Endeavour* and the *Resolution*, and he is also remembered for devising a diet high in Vitamin C, which protected his men against scurvy (the source of the nickname 'limey' for the British). He was murdered in Hawaii.

Robert Falcon Scott (1868–1912, British): failed by a matter of days to become the first person to reach the South Pole, and died, with the rest of his party, in the course of the return journey. One of his companions was Captain Oates, who –

knowing that his weakness was endangering the lives of the others – went out into the blizzard saying, 'I may be some time.'

Roald Amundsen (1872–1928, Norwegian): the one who made it to the South Pole – and back again. He was also the first to sail through the Northwest Passage, the sea route from Pacific to Atlantic along the north coast of North America.

GEOGRAPHY

'Geography is about maps,' said E. Clerihew Bentley, and, although geographers would have a fit at that definition, a lot of what we learned was about the stuff that went on maps. The last section of this chapter should really be classed as palaeontology, but nobody told us that at the time.

Continents and countries of the world

The world is divided into seven continents: Europe, Asia, North America, South America, Africa, Australia and Antarctica. It's a matter of debate to which continent you assign various island nations, as a continent is by definition a land mass. The islands of the Pacific are usually grouped together as 'Oceania', so for the purposes of this list I am going to use that convention and put Australia under that heading, too; and I'm going to create a continent called Central America and include in it all the islands of the Caribbean, as well as the stretch of mainland south of Mexico.

Antarctica contains no countries – instead it is a stateless territory protected from exploitation by an international treaty.

The countries listed here (with their capitals, continents and any change of name since 1945) are the 192 members of the United Nations, the most recent being Montenegro, which divided from Serbia in 2006; Switzerland, that long-term bastion of neutrality, finally succumbed in 2002. They are given in the alphabetical order used by the UN, which provides such delights as The Former Yugoslav Republic of Macedonia coming under 'T'. 'SU' or 'Y' after a country's name means that it was formerly part of the Soviet Union or of Yugoslavia.

COUNTRY	CAPITAL	CONTINENT
Afghanistan	Kabul	Asia
Albania	Tirana	Europe
Algeria	Algiers	Africa
Andorra	Andorra la Vella	Europe
Angola	Luanda	Africa
Antigua & Barbuda	St John's	N. America
Argentina	Buenos Aires	S. America
Armenia (SU)	Yerevan	Asia
Australia	Canberra	Oceania
Austria	Vienna	Europe
Azerbaijan (SU)	Baku	Asia
Bahamas	Nassau	C. America
Bahrain	Manama	Asia
Bangladesh *formerly East Pakistan*	Dhaka	Asia
Barbados	Bridgetown	C. America
Belarus (SU)	Minsk	Europe

COUNTRY	CAPITAL	CONTINENT
Belgium	Brussels	Europe
Belize	Belmopan	C. America
Benin *formerly Dahomey*	Porto Novo	Africa
Bhutan	Thimphu	Asia
Bolivia	La Paz	S. America
Bosnia & Herzegovina (Y)	Sarajevo	Europe
Botswana *formerly Bechuanaland*	Gaborone	Africa
Brazil	Brasilia	S. America
Brunei Darussalam	Bandar Seri Begawan	Asia
Bulgaria	Sofia	Europe
Burkina Faso *formerly Upper Volta*	Ouagadougou	Africa
Burundi *formerly joined with Rwanda to form Ruanda-Urundi*	Bujumbura	Africa
Cambodia *known as Kampuchea from 1976–89*	Phnom Penh	Asia
Cameroon	Yaoundé	Africa
Canada	Ottawa	N. America
Cape Verde	Praia	Africa
Central African Republic	Bangui	Africa
Chad	N'Djamena	Africa
Chile	Santiago	S. America
China	Beijing	Asia
Colombia	Bogota	S. America
Comoros	Moroni	Africa

COUNTRY	CAPITAL	CONTINENT
Congo, Republic of the *formerly the French Congo*	Brazzaville	Africa
Costa Rica	San José	C. America
Côte d'Ivoire *formerly the Ivory Coast*	Yamoussoukro	Africa
Croatia (Y)	Zagreb	Europe
Cuba	Havana	C. America
Cyprus	Nicosia	Europe
Czech Republic *used to be joined to Slovakia to form Czechoslovakia*	Prague	Europe

Democratic People's Republic of Korea *(North Korea to you and me)*	Pyongyang	Asia
Democratic Republic of the Congo *formerly Zaire, before that the Belgian Congo*	Kinshasa	Africa
Denmark	Copenhagen	Europe
Djibouti *formerly the French Territory of the Afars and the Issas*	Djibouti City	Africa
Dominica	Roseau	C. America
Dominican Republic[12]	Santo Domingo	C. America

Ecuador	Quito	S. America

---

12 Easily confused: Dominica is one of the Lesser Antilles islands in the south-eastern Caribbean; the Dominican Republic, further north but still in the Caribbean, shares the island of Hispaniola with Haiti and forms part of the Greater Antilles.

COUNTRY	CAPITAL	CONTINENT
Egypt	Cairo	Africa
El Salvador	San Salvador	C. America
Equatorial Guinea	Malabo	Africa
Eritrea	Asmara	Africa
gained independence from Ethiopia in 1993		
Estonia (SU)	Tallinn	Europe
Ethiopia	Addis Ababa	Africa

Fiji	Suva	Oceania
Finland	Helsinki	Europe
France	Paris	Europe

Gabon	Libreville	Africa
Gambia	Banjul	Africa
Georgia (SU)	Tbilisi	Asia
Germany	Berlin	Europe
from 1949–90 was divided into West (Federal Republic) and East (Democratic Republic), with capitals Bonn and Berlin respectively		
Ghana	Accra	Africa
Greece	Athens	Europe
Grenada	St George's	C. America
Guatemala	Guatemala City	C. America
Guinea	Conakry	Africa
formerly French Guinea		
Guinea-Bissau[13]	Bissau	Africa
formerly Portuguese Guinea		

---

13 Confusingly, next to each other on the Atlantic coast of West Africa.

COUNTRY	CAPITAL	CONTINENT
Guyana *formerly British Guiana*	Georgetown	S. America
Haiti	Port-au-Prince	C. America
Honduras	Tegucigalpa	C. America
Hungary	Budapest	Europe
Iceland	Reykjavik	Europe
India	New Delhi	Asia
Indonesia	Djakarta	Asia
Iran	Tehran	Asia
Iraq	Baghdad	Asia
Ireland	Dublin	Europe
Israel *created in 1948, in an area previously called Palestine*	Jerusalem	Asia
Italy	Rome	Europe
Jamaica	Kingston	C. America
Japan	Tokyo	Asia
Jordan	Amman	Asia
Kazakhstan (SU)	Astana	Asia
Kenya	Nairobi	Africa
Kiribati *formerly Gilbert Islands*	Tarawa	Oceania
Kuwait	Kuwait City	Asia
Kyrgyzstan (SU)	Bishkek	Asia

COUNTRY	CAPITAL	CONTINENT
Laos	Vientiane	Asia
Latvia (SU)	Riga	Europe
Lebanon	Beirut	Asia
Lesotho *formerly Basutoland*	Maseru	Africa
Liberia	Monrovia	Africa
Libya	Tripoli	Africa
Liechtenstein	Vaduz	Europe
Lithuania (SU)	Vilnius	Europe
Luxembourg	Luxembourg City	Europe

Madagascar	Antananarivo	Africa
Malawi *formerly Nyasaland*	Lilongwe	Africa
Malaysia *created in 1963 from the Federation of Malaya, the states of* *Sarawak and Sabah in Borneo and, briefly, Singapore*	Kuala Lumpur	Asia
Maldives	Malé	Asia
Mali *formerly French Sudan*	Bamako	Africa
Malta	Valletta	Europe
Marshall Islands	Delap-Uliga-Darrit	Oceania
Mauritania	Nouakchott	Africa
Mauritius	Port Louis	Africa
Mexico	Mexico City	N. America
Micronesia, Federated States of	Palikir	Oceania
Moldova (SU)	Chisinau	Europe

COUNTRY	CAPITAL	CONTINENT
Monaco	Monaco	Europe
Mongolia	Ulan Bator	Asia
Montenegro (Y)	Podgorica	Europe
Morocco	Rabat	Africa
Mozambique	Maputo	Africa
Myanmar	Nay Pyi Daw	Asia

formerly Burma; the capital until 2006 was Rangoon/Yangon

Namibia	Windhoek	Africa

formerly South West Africa

Nauru	Yaren	Oceania

formerly Pleasant Island

Nepal	Kathmandu	Asia
Netherlands	Amsterdam	Europe
New Zealand	Wellington	Oceania
Nicaragua	Managua	C. America
Niger	Niamey	Africa
Nigeria	Abuja	Africa
Norway	Oslo	Europe

Oman	Muscat	Asia

Pakistan	Islamabad	Asia
Palau	Koror	Oceania

formerly Belau

Panama	Panama City	C. America
Papua New Guinea	Port Moresby	Oceania
Paraguay	Asunción	S. America

COUNTRY	CAPITAL	CONTINENT
Peru	Lima	S. America
Philippines	Manila	Asia
Poland	Warsaw	Europe
Portugal	Lisbon	Europe
Qatar	Doha	Asia
Republic of Korea *(the South)*	Seoul	Asia
Romania	Bucharest	Europe
Russian Federation (SU)	Moscow	Europe/Asia
Rwanda	Kigali	Africa

formerly joined with Burundi to form Ruanda-Urundi

Saint Kitts & Nevis	Basseterre	C. America
Saint Lucia	Castries	C. America
Saint Vincent & the Grenadines	Kingstown	C. America
Samoa	Apia & Pago Pago	Oceania
San Marino	San Marino	Europe
São Tomé & Príncipe	São Tomé	Africa
Saudi Arabia	Riyadh	Asia
Senegal	Dakar	Africa
Serbia (Y)	Belgrade	Europe
Seychelles	Victoria	Africa
Sierra Leone	Freetown	Africa
Singapore	Singapore	Asia

became independent of the Malaysian Federation in 1965

COUNTRY	CAPITAL	CONTINENT
Slovakia	Bratislava	Europe

used to be joined to the Czech Republic to form Czechoslovakia

COUNTRY	CAPITAL	CONTINENT
Slovenia (Y)	Ljubljana	Europe
Solomon Islands	Honiara	Oceania
Somalia	Mogadishu	Africa
South Africa	Pretoria	Africa
Spain	Madrid	Europe
Sri Lanka	Colombo	Asia

formerly Ceylon

COUNTRY	CAPITAL	CONTINENT
Sudan	Khartoum	Africa
Suriname	Paramaribo	S. America

formerly Dutch Guiana

COUNTRY	CAPITAL	CONTINENT
Swaziland	Mbabane	Africa
Sweden	Stockholm	Europe
Switzerland	Berne	Europe
Syria	Damascus	Asia

COUNTRY	CAPITAL	CONTINENT
Tajikistan (SU)	Dushanbe	Asia
Thailand	Bangkok	Asia
The Former Yugoslav Republic of Macedonia	Skopje	Europe
Timor-Leste (East Timor)	Dili	Asia
Togo	Lomé	Africa
Tonga	Nuku'alofa	Oceania
Trinidad & Tobago	Port-of-Spain	C. America
Tunisia	Tunis	Africa
Turkey	Ankara	Europe/Asia
Turkmenistan (SU)	Ashgabat	Asia

COUNTRY	CAPITAL	CONTINENT
Tuvalu *formerly Ellice Islands*	Funafuti	Oceania

Uganda	Kampala	Africa
Ukraine (SU)	Kiev	Europe
United Arab Emirates	Abu Dhabi	Asia
United Kingdom of Great Britain & Northern Ireland	London	Europe
United Republic of Tanzania *formed in 1964 from a union of Tanganyika and Zanzibar*	Dodoma	Africa
United States of America	Washington	N. America
Uruguay	Montevideo	S. America
Uzbekistan (SU)	Tashkent	Asia

Vanuatu *formerly New Hebrides*	Port Vila	Oceania
Venezuela	Caracas	S. America
Vietnam *from 1954–76 divided into North and South, with Hanoi the capital of the North and Saigon (now Ho Chi Minh City) of the South*	Hanoi	Asia

Yemen	San'a	Asia

Zambia *formerly Northern Rhodesia*	Lusaka	Africa
Zimbabwe *formerly Southern Rhodesia, then from 1964–79 Rhodesia; until 1979 the capital was called Salisbury*	Harare	Africa

The United States of America

Listed below are the fifty states with their nicknames, their capitals and the date they entered the Union. Those marked * are the original thirteen 'colonies' that declared themselves independent from British rule in 1776. Those marked ** seceded from the Union during the Civil War and formed the Confederate States of America; all had been readmitted by 1870.

STATE	NICKNAME	CAPITAL	DATE
Alabama **	Yellowhammer State	Montgomery	1819
Alaska	The Last Frontier	Juneau	1959
Arizona	Grand Canyon State	Phoenix	1912
Arkansas **	Natural State	Little Rock	1836
California	Golden State	Sacramento	1850
Colorado	Centennial State	Denver	1876
Connecticut *	Constitution State	Hartford	1788
Delaware*	First State	Dover	1787
Florida **	Sunshine State	Tallahassee	1845
Georgia * and **	Peach State	Atlanta	1788
Hawaii	Aloha State	Honolulu	1959
Idaho	Gem State	Boise	1890

STATE	NICKNAME	CAPITAL	DATE
Illinois	Prairie State	Springfield	1818
Indiana	Hoosier State	Indianapolis	1816
Iowa	Hawkeye State	Des Moines	1846
Kansas	Sunflower State	Topeka	1861
Kentucky	Bluegrass State	Frankfort	1792
Louisiana **	Pelican State	Baton Rouge	1812
Maine	Pine Tree State	Augusta	1820
Maryland *	Old Line State	Annapolis	1788
Massachusetts *	Bay State	Boston	1788
Michigan	Great Lakes State	Lansing	1837
Minnesota	North Star State	St Paul	1858
Mississippi **	Magnolia State	Jackson	1817
Missouri	Show-me State	Jefferson City	1821
Montana	Treasure State	Helena	1889
Nebraska	Cornhusker State	Lincoln	1867
Nevada	Silver State	Carson City	1864
New Hampshire *	Granite State	Concord	1788
New Jersey *	Garden State	Trenton	1787
New Mexico	Land of Enchantment	Santa Fe	1912
New York *	Empire State	Albany	1788
North Carolina * and **	Tar Heel State	Raleigh	1789
North Dakota	Peace Garden State	Bismarck	1889

STATE	NICKNAME	CAPITAL	DATE
Ohio	Buckeye State	Columbus	1803
Oklahoma	Sooner State	Oklahoma City	1907
Oregon	Beaver State	Salem	1859
Pennsylvania *	Keystone State	Harrisburg	1787
Rhode Island *	Ocean State	Providence	1790
South Carolina * and **	Palmetto State	Columbia	1788
South Dakota	Mount Rushmore State	Pierre	1889
Tennessee **	Volunteer State	Nashville	1796
Texas **	Lone Star State	Austin	1845
Utah	Beehive State	Salt Lake City	1896
Vermont	Green Mountain State	Montpelier	1791
Virginia * and **	The Old Dominion	Richmond	1788
Washington	Evergreen State	Olympia	1889
West Virginia	Mountain State	Charleston	1863
Wisconsin	Badger State	Madison	1848
Wyoming	Equality State	Cheyenne	1890

The District of Columbia is a federal district, not a state, sharing its boundaries with the city of Washington, DC.

Mountains

All the mountains in the world that top 8000 metres are in the Himalayas, which is frankly a bit boring for a book like this, but what can you do?

Everest	China/Nepal	8848
K2 (Godley Austen)	China/Kashmir	8611
Kanchenjunga	India/Nepal	8598
Lhotse	China/Nepal	8516
Makalu	China/Nepal	8481
Cho Oyu	China/Nepal	8201
Dhaulagiri	Nepal	8172
Manaslu	Nepal	8156
Nanga Parbut	Kashmir	8126
Annapurna	Nepal	8078
Gasherbrum	China/Kashmir	8068
Broad Peak	China/Kashmir	8051
Xixabangma	China	8012

There are another twenty above 7000 metres, all still in Asia; then we shift to South America for:

Aconagua	Argentina	6960

and nineteen more above 6200 metres, all in the Andes, before it is worth even glancing elsewhere.

Here is a top three from the other continents:

☞ **NORTH AMERICA**

Mount McKinley	USA (Alaska)	6194
Mount Logan	USA	5959
Citlaltepetl	Mexico	5700

☞ **AFRICA**

Kilimanjaro	Tanzania	5895
Mount Kenya	Kenya	5199
Ruwenzori	Uganda/Zaire	5109

☞ **ANTARCTICA**

Vinson Massif	4897
Mount Kirkpatrick	4528
Mount Markham	4349

☞ **EUROPE**

Mont Blanc	France/Italy	4807
Monte Rosa	Italy/Switzerland	4634
Dom	Switzerland	4545

☞ **OCEANIA**

Mount Wilhelm	Papua New Guinea	4508
Aoraki (Mount Cook)	New Zealand	3753[14]
Mount Balbi	Solomon Islands	2439

---

14 When I was at school in New Zealand, Mount Cook – as it was still called – was 3765 metres high (that was 12,349 feet, a nice easy number for us to remember). A massive avalanche in 1991 knocked off twelve metres' worth of rock.

Oceans

The four principal oceans of the world (with areas in thousands of square kilometres) are:

Pacific	179,679
Atlantic	92,373
Indian	73,917
Arctic	14,090

and a top ten of seas:

South China	between mainland Asia & the Philippines	2975
Caribbean	east of Central America	2766
Mediterranean	between Europe and Africa	2516
Bering	at the very north of the Pacific, between Alaska and Russia	2268
Gulf of Mexico	south of the eastern USA, east of Mexico	1543
Sea of Okhotsk	south of eastern Russia, north of Japan	1528
East China & Yellow	east of mainland China, north of the South China and south of the Okhotsk	1249
Hudson Bay	Canada	1232

| Sea of Japan | between Japan and eastern Asia | 1008 |
| North | east of the UK, bounded on the east by Denmark | 575 |

The deepest point in the world is Mariana Trench (in the Pacific, east of the Philippines), at 11,022 metres.

Rivers

The world's longest rivers are more fairly divided than its mountains, so here are the seventeen that are longer than 3500 kilometres, with the countries they mostly flow through:

Nile	Egypt	6670
Amazon	Brazil	6450
Yangtze	China	6380
Mississippi–Missouri	USA	6020
Yenisey–Angara	Russia	5550
Huang He	China	5464
Ob–Irtysh	Russia	5410
Zaire/Congo	Zaire/Congo	4670
Mekong	Vietnam/Cambodia	4500
Paraná–Plate	Argentina	4500
Amur	Russia	4400
Lena	Russia	4400
Mackenzie	Canada	4240
Niger	Nigeria/Niger/Mali	4180
Murray–Darling	Australia	3750

Volga	Russia	3700
Zambezi	Mozambique/	
	Zimbabwe/Zambia	3540

If you counted the Mississippi and Missouri as two separate rivers, they would both still find a place in this list, as would the Ob and Irtysh. The Yenisey on its own would also qualify.

Geological time

The largest subdivision of geological time is an **era**, which can be divided into **periods** and then into **epochs**. The major divisions tend to be marked by mass extinctions, with smaller ones indicated by smaller extinctions and/or climate change. There have been three main eras, with anything earlier than this known as Pre-Cambrian.

☞ PALAEOZOIC ERA, FROM ABOUT 600–250MYA [MILLION YEARS AGO]

The name literally means *ancient life*. Life on Earth had existed for perhaps 4000 million years before this, but it consisted largely of single-celled creatures such as algae and bacteria. The Cambrian period, the first part of the Palaeozoic, is when bigger creatures – some of them crucially with backbones – began to emerge, although they were still living in the sea. The Palaeozoic was followed by the Permian extinction, when ninety-five per cent of all life on Earth – plants and animals, on land and sea, died. Just like that. Just when they were beginning to get the hang of it. (To be fair, the period of extinction lasted millions of years, so 'just like that' is an exaggeration, but scientists still don't know for sure why it happened.)

Anyway, it paved the way for…

☞ MESOZOIC ERA, FROM ABOUT 250–65 MYA

The name means *middle life*. This was the age of the dinosaurs, divided into three periods:

🖋 **Triassic** (*c*.250–220 mya): the time of the first dinosaurs, small and agile to start with but poised to take over the world…
🖋 **Jurassic** (*c*.220–155 mya): when giant herbivores such as *Apatosaurus* (which used to be called Brontosaurus) and *Diplodocus* rule.
🖋 **Cretaceous** (*c*.150–65 mya): the period dominated by *Tyrannosaurus rex*, but also the time when plants first produce flowers.

Then along came the Cretaceous–Tertiary (known as the KT) extinction, when the Earth may or may not have been hit by a meteorite. Nothing like as bad as the Permian but still enough to wipe out the dinosaurs, and following that…

☞ CENOZOIC ERA, FROM ABOUT 65 MYA
TO THE PRESENT

The name means *recent life*. This is when mammals and birds took over. It is sometimes divided into the Tertiary and Quaternary periods, and then subdivided into these epochs:

- **Palaeocene** (65–55 mya): the time when the first large mammals emerge to fill the gaps left by the dinosaurs.
- **Eocene** (55–35 mya): a period of great warmth when the first grasses start to grow.
- **Oligocene** (35–25 mya): great diversification of mammals and flowering plants.
- **Miocene** (25–5.5 mya): the common ancestor of human beings and primates emerges.
- **Pliocene** (5.5–2 mya): that same common ancestor comes down from the trees.
- **Pleistocene** (2 million–11,750 years ago – this is where you enter the Quaternary period if you belong to that school of thought): mammoths and Neanderthal man come and go, but *Homo sapiens* may be here to stay.
- **Holocene** (11,750 years ago–present, but see below): the emergence of agriculture and thus of the first civilizations.

As of early 2008, there is a suggestion that the Holocene period finished in the year 1800, and that human impact since the time of the Industrial Revolution justifies us designating a new period, the Anthropocene, with – to quote the *Times* article on the subject – 'geological records revealing traces of factory pollution, ocean acidification, nuclear testing, greenhouse gases and wildlife extinctions'.

GENERAL STUDIES

It's frowned upon to call a chapter 'Miscellaneous', but this one covers various things that didn't fit in elsewhere: religion, mythology, art, music – all the subjects that you probably didn't do exams in but had to learn a bit of anyway.

World religions

There are, of course, lots of them and lots of subdivisions within them, but here is a little about the five really big ones, starting with the oldest:

☞ JUDAISM

Monotheistic religion whose beginnings are lost in the mists of time. Its adherents are called Jews, their god is eternal and invisible, and trusting in God's will is a fundamental tenet. Jewish law as revealed by God is contained in the Torah, which comprises the first five books of the Christian Old Testament. The Wailing Wall in Jerusalem is a sacred site.

☞ HINDUISM

Polytheistic, about 5000 years old and followed primarily in

India. One of its tenets is that one's actions lead to the reward or punishment of being reincarnated in a higher or lower form of life. The aim is to be freed from this cycle and attain the state of unchanging reality known as Brahman. The three principal creator gods are Brahma, Vishnu and Shiva, but Krishna (an incarnation of Vishnu) is also widely worshipped. The main scriptures are the Vedas. The river Ganges is seen as a goddess of purity and pilgrims come to the holy city of Varanesi (Benares) to bathe in the river. The cow is a sacred symbol of fertility.

☞ BUDDHISM

Founded in the sixth century BC by Gautama Siddhartha, known as the Buddha or 'Awakened One'. There are no gods in Buddhism; its adherents follow the philosophy expressed in the Buddha's Four Noble Truths – that existence is characterized by suffering, that suffering is caused by desire, that to end desire is therefore to end suffering, and that this may be achieved by following the Eightfold Path to the ideal state of nirvana.

☞ CHRISTIANITY

Monotheistic religion that grew out of Judaism 2000 years ago and is based on the belief that Jesus Christ is the son of God. The holy book is the Bible, divided into the Old and New Testaments; the New Testament is the one concerned with the teachings of Christ and his apostles. The church divided initially into Eastern (Orthodox) and Western (Roman Catholic) branches. The Catholic Church still recognizes the Pope as leader and Rome as a holy city but a major rift beginning in the sixteenth century led to the emergence of the Protestants and many subsequent subdivisions. Jerusalem is the traditional site of Christ's burial and resurrection.

☞ ISLAM

Monotheistic religion whose god is called Allah, founded in the seventh century AD by the one prophet, Mohammed. The holy book – the Koran or Qur'an – contains the revelations that Allah made to Mohammed. The holy cities are Mecca, birthplace of Mohammed, and Medina, where he is buried. All able-bodied Muslims who can afford it are expected to make a pilgrimage (*hadj*) to Mecca at least once in their lives. The Dome of the Rock in Jerusalem is the oldest intact Muslim temple in the world and is built over the point from which Mohammed traditionally ascended to heaven.

You'll notice Jerusalem recurring here. That's more or less what the Crusades were about.

☞ THE TEN COMMANDMENTS

Given to Moses by God on Mount Sinai (remember Charlton Heston and those massive tablets?), these are a basic code of conduct for both Jews and Christians.

1 Thou shalt have no other gods before me

2 Thou shalt not make unto thee any graven image, or any likeness of any thing that is in heaven above or that is in the earth beneath, or that is in the water under the earth

3 Thou shalt not take the name of the Lord thy God in vain

4 Remember the Sabbath day and keep it holy

5 Honour thy father and thy mother

6 Thou shalt not kill

7 Thou shalt not commit adultery

8 Thou shalt not steal

9 Thou shalt not bear false witness against thy neighbour

10 Thou shalt not covet thy neighbour's house, thou shalt not covet thy neighbour's wife, nor his manservant, nor his maidservant, nor his ox, nor his ass, nor any thing that is thy neighbour's.

☞ THE SEVEN DEADLY SINS

Not a biblical concept, but established in the Christian tradition by the sixth century and featured in art and literature throughout the Middle Ages. They are:

pride	gluttony	lust	sloth
covetousness	anger	envy	

Roman numerals

I = 1	C = 100
V = 5	D = 500
X = 10	M = 1000
L = 50	

and from there, the Romans could make up any number they wanted – except, interestingly enough, zero, because they didn't have a symbol for it. They made the other numbers by adding (putting letters at the end) or subtracting (putting them at the beginning).

Huh?

OK, for example:
    I = 1
    II = 2
    III = 3
but IV (i.e. one-before-five) = 4

Similarly,
    V = 5
    VI = 6
    VII = 7
    VIII = 8
but IX (one-before-ten) = 9

The same principle applies with the big numbers, so you end up with something like XLIV (44, because it is ten-before-fifty and one-before-four) and CDXCIX (499, made up of one-hundred-before-five-hundred, ten-before-one-hundred and one-before-ten). You would have thought 499 might be ID (one-before-500) but it isn't.

The Seven Wonders of the World

The Seven Wonders of the Ancient World, described in an old encyclopedia as 'remarkable for their splendour or magnitude' were:

The Hanging Gardens of Babylon
The Mausoleum of Halicarnassus
The Pharos (lighthouse) of Alexandria
The Colossus of Rhodes
The Temple of Artemis at Ephesus
The Statue of Zeus at Olympia
The Great Pyramid of Cheops (or Khufu)

Of the seven, only the Pyramid is still in existence.

A bit of classical mythology

There are lots of Greek and Roman gods, and enough mythological characters and demigods to fill a book on their own, but these are some you might remember:

Greek	Roman equivalent	
Zeus	Jupiter	father of the gods, also god of thunder
Hera	Juno	his wife and sister, goddess of marriage (but not, so far as I know, of incest)
Apollo	Apollo	god of hunting and of healing, the god who was consulted at the Oracle of Delphi
Ares	Mars	god of war
Aphrodite	Venus	goddess of love
Artemis	Diana	goddess of hunting and the moon
Hermes	Mercury	messenger of the gods, the one who wore the winged sandals and helmet
Athena	Minerva	goddess of war and of wisdom
Hephaestus	Vulcan	god of fire
Poseidon	Neptune	god of the sea
Demeter	Ceres	goddess of corn and the harvest
Dis	Pluto	god of the underworld

Some famous artists

This was meant to be a Top Twenty, but it kept creeping up – I found I didn't want to leave any of these out.

Sandro Botticelli (1445–1510, Italian): best known for 'The Birth of Venus' (Venus with flowing hair, standing in a shell).

Leonardo da Vinci (1452–1519, Italian): painter, sculptor, inventor and all-round polymath – one of the great figures of the Renaissance. Among many celebrated works are 'Mona Lisa' and 'The Last Supper'.

Michelangelo Buonarotti (1475–1564, Italian): painter – most famously of the ceiling of the Sistine Chapel in the Vatican – and sculptor of the statue of David in Florence.

Raphael (1483–1520, Italian): painter of many versions of the Madonna and Child; and of frescoes, notably 'The School of Athens', for the Sistine Chapel.

Titian (*c.*1490–1576, Italian): greatest painter of the Venetian school: religious and mythological subjects including 'Assumption of the Virgin' and 'Bacchus and Ariadne'.

Hans Holbein the Younger (*c.*1497–1543, German, latterly in England): court painter to Henry VIII, responsible for the flattering portrait of Anne of Cleves that encouraged the king to marry her.

Pieter Brueghel the Elder (1525–69, Flemish): famous for scenes of peasant life and landscapes.

El Greco (Domenikos Theotokopoulos, 1541–1614, Greek living in Spain): used distinctive elongated figures in his paintings of saints and 'The Burial of Count Orgaz'.

Peter Paul Rubens (1577–1640, Flemish): greatest of the Baroque artists, based mainly in Antwerp. Painted the ceiling of the Banqueting Hall in Whitehall, London, but is best remembered for depictions of abundantly fleshy women.

Frans Hals (c.1581–1666, Dutch): painter of 'The Laughing Cavalier'.

Diego de Velázquez (1599–1660, Spanish): court painter to Philip IV, producing many portraits of his patron and his family, notably 'Las Meninas'. Also 'The Rokeby Venus' – the one of her lying naked on a bed, facing away from the viewer and looking at herself in a mirror.

Rembrandt van Rijn (1606–69, Dutch): prolific portraitist and self-portraitist; creator of the vast 'The Night Watch' in the Rijksmuseum in Amsterdam.

Jan Vermeer (1632–75, Dutch): based in Delft, noted for his skilful use of light; painted everyday scenes of women reading or writing letters or playing musical instruments. The subject of *Girl with a Pearl Earring*.

Canaletto (Giovanni Canal, 1697–1768, Italian): famous for his views of Venice, but also spent time in London and painted scenes of the Thames.

William Hogarth (1697–1764, British): engraver; hard-hitting social satires such as 'The Rake's Progress' and 'Gin Lane'.

Francisco de Goya (1746–1828, Spanish): painter, notably of the portraits 'Maja Clothed' and 'Maja Nude', and the dramatic 'Shootings of May 3rd 1808', inspired by Spanish resistance to French occupation.

J(ohn) M(allord) W(illiam) Turner (1775–1851, British): prolific painter of landscapes and maritime scenes, most famously 'The Fighting Téméraire'. His use of colour and light, and his portrayal of weather, anticipated the French Impressionists such as Monet and Renoir.

John Constable (1776–1837, British): painter of landscapes, notably 'The Haywain'.

Edouard Manet (1832–83, French): established before the Impressionists, he adopted some of their techniques but was never quite one of that school. Famous works include 'Déjeuner sur l'Herbe' (the one where the men are fully dressed and the women are not) and 'A Bar at the Folies-Bergère'.

James McNeill Whistler (1834–1903, American, working in England): painter, notably of 'The Artist's Mother'; also known as a wit. He is the one who, when Oscar Wilde remarked, 'How I wish I'd said that' is said to have responded, 'You will, Oscar, you will.'

Edgar Degas (1834–1917, French): Impressionist, the one who painted all those ballet dancers.

Paul Cézanne (1839–1906, French): post-Impressionist and precursor of cubism, based in Provence. In addition to landscapes, famous works include 'The Card Players' and various groups of women bathing.

Claude Monet (1840–1926, French): most important painter of the Impressionist movement, famous for the 'series' paintings that studied the effect of light at different times of day and year on the same subject: Rouen cathedral, haystacks and poplars. Lived latterly at Giverny, outside Paris, now a much-visited garden, and painted a series of the waterlilies (*nymphéas*) there.

Auguste Rodin (1840–1917, French): sculptor, most famously of 'The Kiss', 'The Thinker' and 'The Burghers of Calais'.

Pierre-Auguste Renoir (1841–1919, French): Impressionist, best known for 'Les Parapluies' and 'Le Moulin de la Galette' (a bar in Montmartre).

Paul Gauguin (1848–1903, French): the one who went to Tahiti and painted the people there.

Vincent van Gogh (1853–90, Dutch, working mainly in France): cut off part of his ear and subsequently committed suicide. Self-portraits, 'The Potato Eaters', 'Sunflowers', 'The Starry Night'.

John Singer Sargent (1856–1925, American): portrait painter to the stars, including Ellen Terry, John D. Rockefeller and various young ladies of fashion.

Henri de Toulouse-Lautrec (1864–1901, French): the little one. Lived in Montmartre and painted music halls, cafés and their habitués: works include 'At the Moulin Rouge' and 'La Toilette'.

Pablo Picasso (1881–1973, Spanish, working largely in France): arguably the greatest and certainly the most versatile painter of the twentieth century. After the famous 'rose' and 'blue' periods of his early years, he was fundamental to the development of cubism, expanded the technique of collage, became involved with the surrealists, designed ballet costumes, did a bit of pottery etc, etc. His greatest painting is probably 'Guernica', a nightmarish portrayal of the horrors of the Spanish Civil War.

Salvador Dalí (1914–89, Spanish): surrealist and notable egomaniac. Studied abnormal psychology and dream symbolism and reproduced its imagery in his paintings.

Also worked with the surrealist film director Luis Buñuel (*Le Chien Andalou*) and designed the dream sequence in Alfred Hitchcock's *Spellbound*. His painting of 'The Last Supper' is the one that shows the arms and torso of Christ floating above the disciples at the table.

Jackson Pollock (1912–56, American): abstract expressionist painter who believed that the act of painting was more important than the finished product and whose paintings are therefore highly colourful and chaotic to the point of frenzy. And often huge.

Some famous composers

More disciplined here – my Top Twenty actually has twenty people in it.

Antonio Vivaldi (1678–1741, Italian): composed operas and church music galore, but now mostly remembered for *The Four Seasons*, a suite of violin concertos often played when you ring a call centre and are waiting for an adviser to become available.

Johann Sebastian Bach (1685–1750, German): highly esteemed and vastly influential composer – without him there might have been no Haydn, no Mozart and no Beethoven. Wrote especially organ music, church music and orchestral music: the *Brandenburg Concertos*, the *St Matthew Passion*, *The Well-Tempered Clavier*, *Jesu Joy of Man's Desiring*, lots of good stuff. Came from a famous musical family and had many children, including the composers Carl Philip Emmanuel and Johann Christian; the latter moved to London and became known as 'the English Bach'.

George Frideric Handel (1685–1759, German, working in England): successful in Germany before moving to England when George I became king; wrote the *Water Music* for him. Also wrote a number of operas and developed the English oratorio, of which *Messiah* (which contains the 'Hallelujah Chorus') is the best known; composed the anthem *Zadok the Priest* for the coronation of George II.

Franz Josef Haydn (1732–1809, Austrian): 'Papa Haydn', another vastly prolific composer, credited with the development of the classical symphony (he wrote 104 of them, including the *London* and the *Clock*) and the four-movement string quartet.

Wolfgang Amadeus Mozart (1756–91, Austrian): infant prodigy and all-round genius. Composer of forty-one symphonies, including the *Jupiter*; operas including *Don Giovanni* and *The Magic Flute*; innumerable concertos, sonatas, solo piano pieces and chamber music. Not bad for someone who died at thirty-five.

Ludwig van Beethoven (1770–1827, German): wrote nine symphonies, but the ones we all know are the Fifth (da-da-da-DAH) and the Ninth (the *Choral Symphony*, whose last movement includes the glorious 'Song of Joy' – amazing to think that he was already deaf by this time and never heard it performed). Also wrote *Für Elise*, a piano piece studied laboriously by generations of little girls. And lots of other stuff, including one opera, *Fidelio*.

Gioachino Rossini (1792–1868, Italian): known mostly for operas, including *La Cenerentola, The Barber of Seville* and *William Tell*, which boasts the world's most famous overture.

Franz Schubert (1797–1828, Austrian): lots of people have failed to finish a symphony or two, but when we talk about the *Unfinished Symphony* we tend to mean Schubert's Eighth. He also wrote about 600 songs (*lieder*) and *The Trout* piano quintet (you'd know it if you heard it – I certainly sang it at school).

Frédéric Chopin (1810–49, Polish): wrote some beautiful, tear-jerking stuff for the piano, much of it influenced by Polish folk music: mazurkas, polonaises, waltzes and short romantic pieces called nocturnes, a term he popularized.

Franz Liszt (1811–1886, Hungarian): virtuoso pianist, possibly the best there has ever been, as well as being a prolific composer. His best known works are probably the *Hungarian Rhapsodies*. His daughter Cosima became Mrs Wagner.

Richard Wagner (1813–83, German): the one of whom it was said that he had wonderful moments but bad quarters of an hour. Goodness he could go on. Fans of his work use words like 'masterpiece' and 'greatest achievement in the history of opera', but given that the four 'musical dramas' that comprise the *Ring* cycle run for a total of nearly sixteen hours, I am never going to find out first-hand.

Giuseppe Verdi (1813–1901, Italian): wrote rather shorter operas, notably *Rigoletto, La Traviata, Don Carlos* and *Aida*.

Pyotr Tchaikovsky (1840–93, Russian): best known as a composer of ballet music (*The Nutcracker Suite, Swan Lake, The Sleeping Beauty*), but also wrote the wonderfully loud and patriotic *1812 Overture* after Napoleon had been forced to retreat from Moscow (see p.142).

Edward Elgar (1857–1934, English): responsible for the *Enigma Variations*, including *Pomp and Circumstance* ('Land of Hope and Glory'), without which there could be no Last Night of the Proms.

Giacomo Puccini (1858–1924, Italian): another one for the opera buffs – *La Bohème, Tosca, Madama Butterfly, Turandot*. My reference book says he 'lacks the nobility of Verdi', but makes up for it in dramatic flair and skill. And he certainly wrote tunes.

Arnold Schoenberg (1874–1951, Austrian): wrote rather fewer tunes. Indeed, invented a form of music called 'atonality' and later 'serialism', which are bywords for 'unlistenable-to' with many people.

Gustav Mahler (1860–1911, Austrian): I first heard of him because Tom Lehrer wrote a song about his wife, Alma, but I now know that he was a great conductor and wrote some good music, too. Including nine finished symphonies and an unfinished one, all on a grand scale, and a song-symphony, *Das Lied von der Erde* ('The Song of the Earth').

Gustav Holst (1874–1934, English): best known for the *Planets* suite, which has seven parts, Earth not being deemed worthy of inclusion and Pluto not having been discovered yet. Which is convenient in the light of recent events (see p.190).

Igor Stravinsky (1882–1971, Russian): composed the *Firebird Suite* specifically for Diaghilev's Ballets Russes and followed this with *Petrushka* and *The Rite of Spring*. His style was always experimental, and he turned to neo-classicism and later to serialism, but was never in the same league as Schoenberg for making people reach for the 'off' button.

Sergei Prokofiev (1891–1953, Russian): included because of *Peter and the Wolf*, a 'symphonic fairy tale' that I certainly listened to at school and which crops up on TV every so often. The *Oxford Dictionary of Music* says that it is 'delightful in itself and a wonderful way of instructing children (and others) how to identify orchestral instruments'. My sentiments exactly. I've been scared of the bassoon ever since. Oh, and he wrote other things, too, starting when he was about three: symphonies, ballets (*Romeo and Juliet, Cinderella*), operas, film music (*Alexander Nevsky*) and more.

The planets

When I was at school, this was easy. There were nine planets in our solar system: starting at the sun and working outwards, Mercury, Venus, Earth, Mars, Jupiter, Saturn, Uranus, Neptune and Pluto. And there were sundry mnemonics to help you remember, along the lines of 'My Very Easy Method: Just Set Up Nine Planets'.

Then people kept discovering things. Most importantly, in 2003, they discovered an icy body (that's 'a thing' to you and me – see p.104) that was larger than Pluto, which brought the whole definition of a planet into question. After much controversy, a conference of the International Astronomical Union in 2006 deemed that Pluto no longer qualified. The icy body became known as called Eris – after the Greek goddess of discord, appropriately enough given all the trouble she had caused.

So, there are now officially eight major planets – the first eight on the original list – with Pluto and Eris demoted to the status of minor planets or ice dwarfs. See also *Gustav Holst*, p.189.

BIBLIOGRAPHY

Nicholas Albery, *Poem of the Day* (Sinclair-Stevenson, 1997)

Bill Bryson, *Penguin Dictionary for Writers and Editors*
(Viking, 1991)

Chambers English Dictionary (2003)

Collins English Dictionary (1994)

David Crystal, *The Cambridge Biographical Encyclopedia*
(second edition, 1998)

H. W. Fowler, *A Dictionary of Modern English Usage*
(OUP, revised edition, 1937)

Michael Kennedy, *The Oxford Dictionary of Music* (1994)

The Macmillan Encyclopedia (revised edition, 1989)

Bruce M. Metzer and Michael D. Coogan, *The Oxford Companion
to the Bible* (1993)

Kenneth O. Morgan, *The Oxford Illustrated History of Britain* (1991)

Jenny Olive, *Maths: A Student's Survival Guide* (Cambridge, 2002)

Harold Osborne, *The Oxford Companion to Art* (1970)

Ian Ousby, *The Cambridge Guide to Literature in English*
(revised edition, 1993)

The Oxford Dictionary of Quotations (fourth edition, 1996)

Oxford English Reference Dictionary (1995)

Philip's Concise World Atlas (seventh edition, 1997)

Sir Arthur Quiller-Couch, *The Oxford Book of English Verse*
(1939 edition – my mum won it as a school prize)

The Travel Book (Lonely Planet, 2007)

In addition, www.britishempire.co.uk told me all I needed to
know about British Prime Ministers, http://users.tinyonline.co.uk/
gswithenbank/collnoun.htm told me more than anyone could
possibly need to know about collective nouns, and Wikipedia
provided lots of useful stuff, such as the states of the USA and the
elements of the Periodic Table.

If you've enjoyed *I Used to Know That*, you'll love these other titles from the same series:

 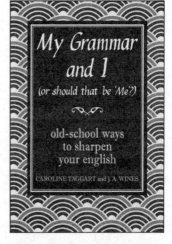

*i before e
(except after c)*
by Judy Parkinson

978-1-84317-249-9

Available in all good
bookshops,
priced £9.99

*My Grammar and I
(or should that be 'Me'?)*
by Caroline Taggart and
J. A. Wines

978-1-84317-310-6

On sale October 2008,
priced £9.99